D0365187

KEYNES, BEVERIDGE

AND BEYOND

KEYNES, BEVERIDGE AND BEYOND

Tony Cutler
Karel Williams
and
John Williams

Routledge & Kegan Paul
London and New York

First published in 1986 by
Routledge & Kegan Paul Ltd
11 New Fetter Lane, London EC4P 4EE

Published in the USA by
Routledge & Kegan Paul Inc.
in association with Methuen Inc.
29 West 35th Street, New York, NY 10001

Set in Baskerville 10/11pt
and printed in Great Britain
by Butler & Tanner Ltd
Frome and London

Library of Congress Cataloguing in Publication Data

Cutler, Tony.

Keynes, Beveridge, and beyond.

Bibliography: p.
Includes index.
1. Great Britain——Economic policy——1945– .
2. Welfare state. 3. Keynes, John Maynard, 1883–1946.
4. Beveridge, William Henry Beveridge, Baron, 1879–1963.
5. Collectivism. 6. Liberalism. I. Williams, Karel.
II. Williams, John (John L.)   III. Title.
HC256.5.C87   1986   338.941   86–11851

British Library CIP Data also available

ISBN 0–7102–0483–3 (c)
ISBN 0–7102–0992–4 (p)

Contents

Figures

Tables

Note and acknowledgments

Discussion amongst three friends in the summer of 1984 led to the notion of a book on economic and social trends which would take as its starting-point the works of the two main architects of the post-war socio-economic system. *Keynes, Beveridge and Beyond* represents the result. It has been collaboratively written. We worked jointly on the research and drafting of each of the chapters.

We owe a considerable debt to Rosemary Law who cheerfully and quickly typed successive drafts whilst continuing to cope with all her other duties as departmental secretary.

Tony Cutler   Middlesex Polytechnic
Karel Williams } University College of
John Williams } Wales, Aberystwyth

Introduction

There have been many histories of British economic and social policy since 1945. There is also an increasing number of economics texts on the 'British economic crisis' which is caused by poor manufacturing performance. We have points to make on these themes and hope that our book will be useful to those who study them. At the same time, we would claim that the main objective of our project is a new and different one. Our aim has been to write the history of a political *a priori* which we call liberal collectivism and which we assert is central to the understanding of economic and social policy in post-war Britain.

The first task of the book is thus to define the concept of liberal collectivism. We then go on to demonstrate that the assumptions of liberal collectivism, formulated in the 1930s and 1940s, were enormously influential after 1945; they formed the tacit basis of the post-war policy settlement and government commitment to the welfare state and full employment. Finally, we look at the limitations of liberal collectivism, both inherent and as a response to the actual post-war experience, and propose some new departures.

The definition of liberal collectivism is established from an analysis of the major works of its two chief architects: Beveridge and Keynes. There are several essential components. Liberal collectivism requires that a social commitment be made to certain minimal objectives which are seen as a condition of existence for a liberal society. Keynes and Beveridge saw poverty and economic insecurity, for example, as dysfunctional and ultimately threatening to the continuance of the capitalist order. Both experience and theory indicated that the abolition of these evils could not be attained without state intervention in a liberal market economy. Thus Keynes and Beveridge never accepted traditional laissez-faire hostility to state intervention.

The liberal collectivist position on state intervention is distinctive because it recommends necessary, but minimal, state intervention. If state intervention to safeguard basic norms is necessary, it should be circumscribed so that there is as little interference as possible with the valuable political and economic freedoms of capitalism. Paradox-

1

ically, appropriate intervention can re-establish the conditions of existence of such liberties (elsewhere); for example, state intervention ensuring full employment would allow the flourishing of both private consumption and saving in the unregulated market sphere.

We should make it clear that our aim was not only to analyse but also to develop a critique of liberal collectivism which develops three critical theses. First, there were inherent flaws in the original liberal collectivist design of the 1930s and 1940s which falsely promised the best of both worlds with as much planning as necessary and as much capitalist freedom as possible. Second, the liberal collectivist programme was increasingly undermined by changing economic and social circumstances in the long boom of the 1950s and 1960s and the rolling recession and slump of the 1970s and 1980s. Third, we would argue that, if we are to solve our worsening economic and social problems, then it is necessary to break with the problem definitions and policy prescriptions of liberal collectivism.

Given these objectives, the organisation of the book is straightforward. The first chapter analyses the nature of liberal collectivism and its inherent limitations. Our second and third chapters concentrate on establishing the increasing irrelevance of liberal collectivism in the post-war world. And the fourth and final chapter establishes how our current economic crisis is not amenable to a liberal collectivist solution.

In the first chapter we establish the features of the liberal collectivist problematic by analysing two key texts – Keynes's *General Theory* of 1936 and Beveridge's *Social Insurance and the Allied Services* of 1942. This is appropriate because Keynes and Beveridge were the architects, if not the only begetters, of liberal collectivism. Most of this chapter is concerned with the problem definitions and solutions proposed in these texts.

At the level of problem definition, Keynes and Beveridge carefully construct economic and social problems which are caused by limited, remediable malfunctions in a capitalist market system. For Keynes, unemployment is not caused by the accumulation of capital or a falling rate of profit but by psychological problems about the inducement to invest. For Beveridge, poverty is caused not by a fundamental maldistribution of income but by a problem of 'interruption of earnings'.

With the problems circumscribed in this way, minimalist intervention can be proposed with some assurance that it would be effective. In 1936 Keynes proposed socialisation of investment and he was later converted to demand management: neither policy required socialist interference with the ownership of the means of production. In 1942 Beveridge proposed flat-rate social insurance which would raise all workers to the poverty line without interfering with the broader distribution of incomes above that line.

While such interventions were politically congenial for the liberal collectivists, we would argue they were always Utopian. Keynes did not see that his socialisation of investment policy threatened the privilege of the capitalist owning class who would resist in the traditional way with gilts strike and capital flight. Beveridge's flat-rate .insurance scheme was quite unlike the graduated continental European insurance systems; it was financed by a regressive poll tax on the working class which produced a limited contribution base.

If Beveridge is now remembered as the author of a social insurance scheme, he was equally concerned with private provision above the minimum which was analysed in an important but neglected text of 1948. *Voluntary Action* argued that the motive of mutual aid operating through voluntary associations like friendly societies could play a major role in providing private welfare above the state minimum. As chapter 2 argues, in the event, the sphere of private welfare was increasingly dominated by a system of occupational cum fiscal welfare where occupational pensions, company cars and mortgage tax relief were powerful accelerators of inequality.

To illustrate this theme, in chapter 2 we consider the post-war development of company pensions which are the most important form of occupational welfare. We show how occupational pensions schemes expanded rapidly in the 1950s and 1960s to take in half the workforce. Chapter 2 then analyses how private pension schemes promote inequality. They systematically reward the well-paid, male, middle-class employee of the large corporation and disadvantage the poorly paid, women, manual workers and those who work for small firms.

Chapter 2's analysis stems from Richard Titmuss's seminal work on the social division of welfare in the 1950s and 1960s. Although Titmuss confined himself to social policy and concentrated on right-wing critics of the welfare state, his work anticipates our criticism of liberal collectivism. All we have added is an insistence on the necessity for settling accounts with Beveridge who was the liberal collectivist architect of the social security system that was under attack from the right in the 1950s and 1960s.

Chapter 3 takes up the theme of the Keynesian pursuit of full employment in the post-war world. The problem of the means by which full employment might be maintained was never resolved by Keynes or by official documents such as the 1944 White Paper, and the Keynesians were necessarily irrelevant when unemployment became an issue in the 1970s. At the same time we should emphasise that the main thrust of our argument in chapter 3 is concerned with the composition of employment rather than the level of employment.

By composition of employment we mean the pattern of employment by gender, skill and pay level which the economy requires and generates. We demonstrate that the original texts of liberal collectivism made strong assumptions about the composition of employment: male heads of working-class families would easily find manual work in the manufacturing sector while their wives concentrated on what Beveridge called the 'vital but unpaid labour' of child rearing.

The empirical sections of chapter 3 show how these assumptions have been invalidated by the experience of the past thirty years. In this period we have lost more than three million manufacturing jobs and gained a similar number of service jobs. We emphasise that this shift has significant welfare implications as ill-paid, part-time jobs are substituted for relatively well-paid full-time jobs.

Increasingly acute problems about the composition of employment are generated by the decline of British manufacturing, whose uncompetitiveness has become steadily more obvious since the 1950s. Many accept that we face an economic crisis when the oil runs out. Chapter 4 develops the argument that the crisis will come more quickly: the rapidly increasing deficit on our trade in manufactures will create a payments crisis before the end of the decade. It is also argued that conventional micro and macro policy instruments are inadequate to deal with this coming foreign trade crisis.

As the case of British cars shows, many enterprises now face fundamental problems which management cannot resolve at the level of the enterprise. As the case of Japan shows, industrial policy cannot solve our problems because in that country it is the organisation of production and marketing which makes the industrial policy work. In orthodox macro policy terms, we are also boxed in: reflation will not work because of the leakage of purchasing power abroad. At the same time, chapter 4 argues positively that we can control the crisis if we reject free trade: selective import controls on cars and consumer electronics can help avert the coming trade crisis.

Our criticism of classic liberal collectivism relents at this point. We show, for example, that Keynes would almost certainly have sanctioned deviation from free trade in our present circumstances where it is against the national interest. More broadly, we accept that in the 1930s and 1940s liberal collectivism was a progressive force for establishing new standards of welfare through the control of unemployment and poverty. But it has now ossified into a dogma which is a reactionary obstruction to appropriate economic policies and, in the sphere of the social, an excuse for more cuts.

If liberal collectivism has failed, what options are there beyond liberal collectivism? In the sphere of economic policy, the road must lead to control over the operation of the market, both domestically and internationally; this means the development of domestic policies of economic planning and international policies of import controls. In the sphere of social policy the need is for the development of policies which tackle the whole range of income and wealth inequalities rather than simply combating 'poverty'. It is not the aim of this book to detail how such policies might operate. Our aim is to problematise liberal collectivism and thus to show the necessity for putting such policies at the top of a new agenda.

1 Beveridge and Keynes: defining liberal collectivism

This chapter compares two key texts by Beveridge and Keynes. The analysis of the social in *Social Insurance and the Allied Services* and the theory of the economy in the *General Theory* are, of course, different in many respects. Our thesis is that, despite these differences, the key texts are similar in that they share a common political *a priori*. Before we establish and develop this thesis, it is useful to begin by outlining the very different character of the two texts.

Social Insurance and the Allied Services (Beveridge, 1942, hereafter *SIAS*) was a government White Paper on what would now be called 'the reform of social security'. It was resolutely empirical in its approach: 'The plan is based on a diagnosis of want. It starts from facts, from the condition of the people as revealed by social surveys between the wars' (*SIAS*, p. 8). Beveridge culled two main conclusions from these local surveys of social conditions in London and some major provincial towns. First, a substantial minority of the working-class population lived in 'want', below the subsistence poverty lines set in these surveys. Second, there was one major cause of such poverty; three-quarters or more of it was caused by 'interruption or loss of earning power' (*SIAS*, p. 7).

Beveridge's report proposed to abolish such poverty; 'the Plan for Social Security ... takes abolition of want after this war as its aim' (*SIAS*, p. 8). *SIAS* also envisaged that 'the provision of an income should be associated with treatment designed to bring the interruption of earnings to an end as soon as possible' (*SIAS*, p. 120), and the corollary of treatment was most strongly developed in Beveridge's proposal for a comprehensive National Health Service (*SIAS*, pp. 157–63). But, given the emphasis on the income deficiency of those below the poverty line, it was quite logical that Beveridge was primarily concerned with proposals for income maintenance.

Beveridge's position on state income maintenance was distinctive since he envisaged that 'compulsory social insurance' could and should do most of the work. The pre-1914 Liberal reforms had introduced state health and unemployment insurance which were then developed in the inter-war period. *SIAS* proposed to abolish poverty by raising insurance contributions and paying out substantially higher benefits; 'social insurance should aim at guaranteeing the minimum income needed for subsistence' (*SIAS*, p. 14). At the same time, *SIAS* proposed a more comprehensive social insurance scheme which would eliminate the gaps in the existing schemes. The whole population (including self-employed, high-paid and dependants of various kinds) would be covered in the new scheme (*SIAS*, pp. 9–10). All the major misfortunes and contingencies which constituted 'primary causes of need' would be covered by some kind of insurance benefit; the list included unemployment, disability, loss of livelihood, retirement, marriage needs, funeral expenses, childhood, physical disease or incapacity (*SIAS*, p. 125). The basic insurance benefits were to be indefinite in duration; a weekly cash allowance would be paid as long as the interruption of earnings lasted (*SIAS*, p. 11, pp. 57–9). None of the insurance allowances were to be means-tested; a weekly cash allowance would be paid automatically to all who could establish their status as sick, unemployed, etc. and the fact of contribution (*SIAS*, p. 120).

The *General Theory* (Keynes, 1936, hereafter *GT*) is a text on what Keynes in the preface called 'difficult questions of theory'. The policy recommendations are underdeveloped and take the form of throw-away asides, as in the concluding paragraphs of chapter 10, supplemented by the ambiguities of the famous final chapter 24. Most of the text elaborates a 'pure theory of what determines the actual employment of the available resources' in a (more or less) closed capitalist national economy. Such theory necessarily addresses abstract questions at a very rarefied level and in the case of the *GT* this tendency is reinforced by an explicit retreat from the realm of the observable and measurable. In chapter 4, for example, Keynes insists that a theoretical understanding of the variation in employment and output is possible although he cannot solve practical problems about conceptualising or measuring the quantity of capital or the general price level. Or, again, Keynes makes new investment depend on the 'marginal efficiency of capital' (business expectations of prospective yield). In many ways this is the key independent variable in the Keynesian system and, significantly, it is not measurable or directly observable.

Keynes offers a theory of demand-led fluctuations in employment and output which explains how aggregate effective demand is usually deficient and why consequently unemployment is the norm in capitalist national economies. This theory of deficient demand analyses demand into two components – consumption and investment expenditure. Consumer expenditure is chronically deficient because the marginal propensity to consume is less than one; 'when aggregate real income is increased, aggregate consumption is increased, but not by as much as income' (*GT*, p. 27). This kind of steady-state underconsumption requires the compensation of new investment expenditure if aggregate demand sufficient for full employment is to be maintained. But new investment expenditure does not steadily compensate because it switches on and off according to how the marginal efficiency of capital (or volatile business expectations of profit from new investment) fluctuates above and below a conventional rate of interest. To sum up,

> a relatively weak propensity to consume helps to cause
> unemployment, by requiring and *not* receiving the accompaniment
> of a compensating volume of new investment which, even if it may
> sometimes occur temporarily through errors of optimism, is in
> general prevented from happening at all by the prospective profit
> falling below the standard set by the rate of interest. (*GT*, p. 370)

The presentation of the *GT*'s theory of unemployment is complicated because the text is written partly in the form of a critique of 'classical economics'. The main theoretical object of attack is the marginalist theory of unemployment (as developed in the 1930s by A. C. Pigou) which attributes the phenomenon of unemployment to sticky money wages. On this view, unemployment exists because organised workers have demanded and obtained a wage which is greater than their marginal product justifies. The *GT* makes a double attack on this marginalist explanation. Negatively, in chapters 2 and 3, Keynes dissects and criticises the logical confusions and conceptual imprecisions of the marginalist explanation of unemployment. Positively, Keynes advances an alternative explanation which attributes unemployment to deficient aggregate demand which arises, as we have seen, because a general propensity to underconsumption is not steadily compensated for by new investment. As chapter 19 makes clear, this alternative explanation cannot be reduced to marginalism because the causal relations between the old marginalist variables are changed at the same time as the Keynesian theory introduces new variables which are not conceptualised in the marginalist scheme (*GT*, p. 278). Thus, in the *GT*, real wages are identified as a dependent variable proximately determined by the volume of employment, while Keynes introduces new system-determining independent variables in the form of the 'marginal propensity to consume' and the 'marginal efficiency of capital'.

The accounts of the *GT* and *SIAS* so far only demonstrate the radical difference of the two texts. It will now be argued that the texts are similar insofar as they share a common political *a priori*. Beveridge and Keynes are separately engaged on the common task of re-inventing liberalism; they reject the old liberal *laissez-faire* position of general hostility to state intervention in a market economy. With the presumption against state intervention suspended, the task of the new liberal is to make a reasoned demarcation of the proper sphere of state action. In making this demarcation, liberal collectivists like Beveridge and Keynes take up certain characteristic positions which constitute the fundamental features of the *a priori*.

(i) Certain basic conditions of social life have to be ensured. Poverty and economic insecurity, for example, are dysfunctional and may ultimately threaten the existence of the capitalist order.

(ii) The maintenance of these conditions of social life is impossible on the free market if a policy of strict *laissez-faire* is pursued. The control of poverty, for example, requires some form of state social security and so does the curbing of insecurity.

(iii) State intervention is not undesirable but imperatively necessary. This is because norms on the basic conditions of social life cannot be maintained without some form of state intervention.

(iv) State intervention should be minimal and confined to what is necessary. Intervention should be circumscribed in nature and extent so that there is as little interference as possible with the valuable political and economic freedoms of capitalism.

(v) State intervention should be directed so that it suppresses basic capitalist freedoms only so as to re-establish the conditions of their effective functioning (elsewhere). Classically, for example, with state regulation established in one sphere of the economy, unregulated market choice can flourish elsewhere.

Ultimately, the new liberal position is distinctive because it recommends large slabs of collectivism in the interests of preserving as much as possible of capitalist individualism. The liberal collectivists accepted the traditional philosophical justification of capitalism as a political and economic system whose virtue is that it leaves a man free to do what he wills with his own. At the same time, the liberal collectivists accepted that the consequences of this freedom on the market were entirely unacceptable and these consequences would have to be curbed by state intervention in some respects if capitalist freedoms were to survive more generally.

With the main features of the political *a priori* sketched, the next major task is to demonstrate that this *a priori* runs through the problem definitions and policy recommendations in *SIAS* and the *GT*. Although the *a priori* has been defined above mainly in terms of policy recommendations, it can only be established in the economic or the social on the basis of an appropriate problem definition; the initial criticism of the capitalist system has to be limited so that the problem which intervention has to solve is not fundamental to, and inherent in, the capitalist order. As for policy recommendations, here it is simply a question of tracing how the texts propose politically congenial interventions which are the minimum necessary to deal with the diagnosed problems.

The political a priori in *SIAS*

As we have noted, Beveridge's aim was to abolish poverty. In proposing this aim, *SIAS* depended on an object and on an operational measure of poverty which were borrowed from the inter-war social surveys. Both the object and the operational measure are of considerable political significance.

Beveridge needs the social scientific object of poverty because it demarcates a limited sphere of state action. Poverty focuses attention on the issue of a deficiency of income at the bottom end of the range of distribution and it diverts attention from the issue of inequality and the whole distribution of incomes from top to bottom. More specifically, poverty allows Beveridge to take up a series of classic liberal collectivist positions. Poverty represents a problem of maldistribution of income which cannot be rectified on the free market through the mechanism of rising real incomes,

> growing general prosperity and rising wages diminished want, but did not reduce want to insignificance. The moral is that new measures to spread prosperity are needed. The plan for social security is designed to meet this need. (*SIAS*, p. 166)

At the same time, poverty sets up a distributional problem which can be rectified without upsetting the whole range of income inequalities. Indeed, according to *SIAS*, inter-class redistribution would be diversionary,

> correct distribution does not mean what it has often been taken to mean in the past – distribution between the different agents of production, between land, capital, management and labour. Better distribution of purchasing power is required among wage earners themselves, as between times of earning and not earning and between times of heavy family responsibilities and of light or no family responsibilities. (*SIAS*, p. 167)

Beveridge quite explicitly stopped short of recommending that redistribution should be confined to the working class but he could not resist making the point that redistribution could be confined to the working class; the social surveys of the 1930s showed that the income surplus of working-class families above the poverty line was very much larger than the income deficit of those below the poverty line and the implication was that 'want could have been abolished before the present war by a redistribution of income within the wage-earning classes'. (*SIAS*, p. 165)

To sustain the poverty problem definition and carry it through to policy recommendations, Beveridge needed an appropriate operational measure of poverty. *SIAS* therefore privileged the kind of calculation of minimum necessary income which was pioneered by Rowntree in his 1899 York Survey and which was then reworked by Rowntree and others in the inter-war poverty surveys. In the poverty surveys this calculation defined a poverty line below which households lacked the minimum necessary income; in *SIAS* the calculation specified a target up to which the state income maintenance system would provide support.

The necessary income calculation costed rent, food, clothing, heating, household necessaries and sundries and then added a margin to allow for inefficiency and waste. The calculation left major problems unresolved. It did not represent a bare subsistence minimum because the calculation made concessions to cultural patterns of consumption which pushed up expenditure; in *SIAS*, for example, expenditure on food was based on League of Nations and British Medical Association dietaries which included meat although vegetarianism was a more economical alternative for the working class. But the concessions were never taken to the point where they accommodated actual consumption patterns. This is most clear in the *SIAS* treatment of rent and 'waste' where the concessions are arbitrarily limited. Beveridge proposed a rent allowance (10/- or 50p a week in 1938 prices) which was pitched slightly below the average for all industrial households as revealed in a Ministry of Labour survey of 1937–8. *SIAS* ignored the marked local and regional variation in the rents actually paid; in the highest rent area of London industrial households paid rents which were over 50 per cent higher than the national average (*SIAS*, p. 78). The treatment of 'wasteful' expenditure was equally striking. *SIAS* proposed an allowance of 2/- (10p) a week for a man and wife in 1938 prices to cover inefficient purchasing and diversion of expenditure on to non-essentials (*SIAS*, p. 87). This was rather half-hearted when the average working-class family in the 1930s spent 7/- (35p) per week on drink alone (Rowntree, 1942, p. 493).

As an attempt to define an adequate minimum income level, Beveridge's calculation is thoroughly incoherent and unsatisfactory; *SIAS* never establishes that it is possible to provide realistically for a family on such an income. But to abuse the calculation on this account is to miss the point because the calculation has a political rationale. The procedures of the poverty surveys do not function as a scientific point of departure but as a politically congenial point of support for liberal collectivism. A (scientifically unspecifiable) minimum income level is

politically important to *SIAS* because it defines the target at which
state income maintenance should be aimed.

The question of how the state reaches this target is equally important. Indeed, the political *a priori* is most strongly developed in Beveridge's discussion of the form which income maintenance should take.
As we have already noted, *SIAS* envisaged a social security system
which was dominated by 'compulsory social insurance'. Non-contributory assistance was to be a 'subsidiary method' (*SIAS*, p. 103)
which would deal with the relatively small and diminishing number
of 'special cases' (*SIAS*, pp. 120–1) who did not qualify for insurance
benefit. Beveridge was an insurance freak of long standing whose
enthusiasm is epitomised by the title of his 1924 pamphlet, 'Insurance
for all and everything'. Why did *SIAS* recommend the social insurance
technique?

Compulsory social insurance was fiscally expedient because it represented a way of recovering 'a substantial part of the cost of benefit as
a contribution' (*SIAS*, p. 12). The alternative was a non-contributory
social security system which was financed entirely out of increased
general taxation. This alternative was technically problematic in 1942
when the PAYE system (for cumulative withholding of tax out of
current income) was a wartime innovation and when it was not clear
whether the working classes would pay income tax after the war was
over. If the tax base for non-contributory social security was likely to
be limited, the results of such a system might also perhaps be more
radically redistributive; as Beveridge well knew, social insurance promoted limited redistribution because the employer's contribution was
a 'tax on employment' and the employee's contribution a regressive
'poll tax' on working-class incomes (*SIAS*, p. 155).

With these dedicated revenue sources, social insurance could operate on principles which were different from those of private insurance
(*SIAS*, pp. 12–13). Under Beveridge's scheme, there was to be no
adjustment of premiums for individual risk (*SIAS*, p. 35); 'no individual should be entitled to claim better terms because he is healthier
or in more regular employment' (*SIAS*, p. 30). Equally, under Beveridge's scheme, the payment of benefits would not be secured by the
accumulation of a reserve fund (*SIAS*, pp. 12–13); the state could
finance an unfunded scheme on a 'pay as you go basis' whereby this
year's contributions paid for this year's benefits. Finally, actuarial
techniques were not used to determine the relation between contributions and benefits. Under Beveridge's scheme an actuarial
relation was impossible because the state was committed to paying
subsistence benefits indefinitely without any contributory conditions
(*SIAS*, p. 140).

But we should not conclude from all this that social insurance in
SIAS is an empty fiction which simply conceals a convenient form of

taxation. The technique of social insurance advocated in *SIAS* has certain specific characteristics: a dedicated insurance contribution in the form of the employee's stamp is paid into a specific insurance fund from which those who satisfy the status requirements (as sick, old, unemployed, etc.) draw a benefit as of right. These characteristics are politically valuable to a liberal collectivist like Beveridge because they transform the 'social' relation between the individual and the state. The technique of social insurance has a negative value because its characteristics limit the possibility of dependence and a positive value because they maximise the possibility of independence.

To begin with, *SIAS* argues that the state's response to poverty should not take the form of a philanthropy which offers gifts to the needy,

> whatever money is required for provision of insurance benefits ... should come from a Fund to which the recipients have contributed and to which they may be required to make larger contributions if the Fund proves inadequate.... The insured persons should not feel that income for idleness, however caused, can come from a bottomless purse. (*SIAS*, p. 12)

The possibility of demoralised dependence is reduced by social insurance because the individual as contributor acquires an interest in economical administration:

> The citizens as insured persons should realise that they cannot get more than certain benefits for certain contributions, should have a motive to support measures for economic administration, should not be taught to regard the State as the dispenser of gifts for which no one needs to pay. (*SIAS*, p. 108)

More than this, the fact of individual contribution through a working life in return for the right to state benefit establishes a new kind of social contract between the state and the individual citizen. Income maintenance is no longer an unconditional gift but a conditional exchange:

> The plan is not one for giving to everybody something for nothing and without trouble, or something that will free the recipients for ever thereafter from personal responsibilities. The plan is one to secure income for subsistence on condition of service and contribution and in order to make and keep men fit for service. (*SIAS*, p. 170)

Insofar as the unconditional dole gift was replaced by a qualified insurance entitlement, the new social contract increased rather than diminished personal responsibility. For example, individuals who became unemployed or sick would in future be under an obligation to make themselves fit for further service.

> The correlative of the State's undertaking to ensure adequate benefit for unavoidable interruption of earnings, however long, is enforcement of the citizen's obligation to seek and accept all reasonable opportunities of work, to co-operate in measures designed to save him from habituation to idleness and to take all proper measures to be well. (*SIAS*, p. 58)

If social insurance limited dependence, the right form of social insurance could also more positively promote independence. To begin with, contributory social insurance could dispense with the means tests which, in Britain and elsewhere, had been widely used as a way of curtailing expenditure on non-contributory social security. *SIAS* did not resist means tests for the modern pragmatic reason that such tests discouraged applicants and produced problems about 'take-up' of benefits. From Beveridge's liberal point of view, means tests were politically objectionable because they discouraged the private savings or voluntary insurance which were necessary if the sphere of social independence was to be as large as possible. As *SIAS* observed, for example, in a discussion of the needs of the long-term sick and unemployed, 'The needs of persons suffering from prolonged unemployment and disability are ... for as much income at least as before without any means test discouraging voluntary provision' (*SIAS*, p. 57).

This solicitude for promoting independence emerges even more clearly if we examine the form of *flat-rate* social insurance which *SIAS* recommended. Appendix F on 'comparisons with other countries' admitted that, although the British had favoured flat-rate contributions and benefits since 1911, graduated earnings-related social insurance schemes were the norm in other countries. Only Eire, which had inherited the British system, operated a flat-rate system while New Zealand had graduated tax contributions for flat-rate benefits. In practical terms, British-type flat-rate contributions put a severe constraint on the scope of benefits. Since the flat-rate contributions were regressive, there was a limit to how far they could be pushed (*SIAS*, p. 155); given restraints on the exchequer contributions to the insurance fund, flat-rate contributions meant severe restrictions on benefit levels and/or coverage. But this was not a problem for Beveridge because he believed in the political desirability of a flat-rate state benefit system which paid the subsistence minimum income and not a penny more:

> The State in organising security should not stifle incentive, opportunity, responsibility; in establishing a national minimum,

it should leave room and encouragement for voluntary action by each individual to provide more than that minimum for himself and his family. (*SIAS*, pp. 6–7)

This division of responsibility in income maintenance had a liberal collectivist rationale of a quite explicit kind. State intervention was to be circumscribed so as to preserve as much as possible of the capitalist freedom of the individual to do what he will with his own,

> to give by compulsory insurance more than is needed for subsistence is an unnecessary interference with individual responsibilities. More can be given only by taking more in contributions or taxation. That means departing from the principle of a national minimum, above which citizens shall spend their money freely, and adopting instead the principle of regulating the lives of individuals by law. (*SIAS*, p. 118)

Of course, the subsistence minimum had to be financed by insurance contributions which were a compulsory deduction from wages. But Beveridge was prepared to tolerate this incursion on the wage earner's freedom because it could re-establish the conditions of capitalist freedom elsewhere above the state minimum. *SIAS* assumed that many wage earners would choose responsibly to make 'supplementary provision' above the state minimum either by saving or by taking out some form of voluntary insurance. The latter could indeed find a new role 'beyond subsistence level in meeting general risks, by adding to the amount of compulsory benefits' (*SIAS*, p. 143). This position did not represent an expedient concession to powerful private interests. There were some areas of growth notably in superannuation and hospital schemes (*SIAS*, p. 160), but unemployment insurance through trade unions was virtually extinct and friendly societies had grown very slowly so that they had just five and a half million enrolled members in 1939. In this situation, Beveridge aimed to encourage a new growth of voluntary provision for reasons of political principle. The liberal collectivism which established a subsistence minimum through social insurance would at the same time re-establish the conditions of individualism through voluntary insurance. Thus it was not at all paradoxical to conclude, 'Voluntary insurance to supplement compulsory insurance is an integral feature of the Plan for Social Security' (*SIAS*, p. 33).

If the political *a priori* is therefore determinant in the overall design of a flat-rate insurance scheme, it is equally notable that Beveridge rigorously follows through and works out the logic of his political position in the discussion of details about entitlement and benefit levels. We can demonstrate this point by examining the *SIAS* treatment of three issues in this area – entitlement to family allowances; differentiation of long- and short-term benefit rates; and uniformity of benefit in sickness and unemployment. As we shall see, the crucial consideration in each case is not the provision of adequate subsistence benefits but the maximising of personal responsibility and the maintenance of the conditions of social independence. In many ways, Beveridge approaches the different issues by coherently applying one political principle: 'the higher the benefits provided out of a common fund for unmerited misfortune, the higher must be the citizen's sense of obligation not to draw upon the fund unnecessarily' (*SIAS*, p. 58). This sense of obligation was to be enforced by the detailed design of entitlements within an appropriate social insurance system.

For Beveridge, provision for children should ideally come within the ambit of social insurance; 'it can be argued that ... children are a contingency for which all men should prepare by contributing to an insurance fund' (*SIAS*, p. 155). But, given a limited (flat-rate) revenue base and the other expenditure demands on the insurance fund, Beveridge recognised that it was not feasible to fund children's allowances 'to any extent' out of the insurance fund (*SIAS*, p. 155). If children's allowances had to be financed on a non-contributory basis from general taxation, measures had to be taken to affirm personal responsibility. Beveridge proposed that child allowance should not be paid on the first child where a parent was in work. This decision was not entirely motivated by Treasury parsimony; there was an explicit political rationale for an allowance system which did not cover the costs of raising a family of two or three children:

> When the responsible parent (that is to say the parent on whom
> the children depend) is earning, there is no need to aim at
> allowances relieving the parent of the whole cost of the children.
> On the view taken here, it would be wrong to do so – an
> unnecessary and undesirable inroad on the responsibilities of
> parents. (*SIAS*, pp. 155–6)

In the *SIAS* treatment of long- and short-term benefit rates, the consideration of subsistence adequacy is equally clearly subordinated for similar political reasons. On a subsistence basis it is easy to argue the need for higher long-term rates which cover renewals of durables like shoes, clothing, furniture, pots and pans, etc. Beveridge recognises this point when he is calculating necessary expenditure:

> Strictly, the figures for clothing and one or two minor items relate
> only to short periods of unemployment and disability during which
> expenditure on renewals can be postponed; more will be needed
> in prolonged interruption of earnings. (*SIAS*, p. 87)

But Beveridge does not recommend higher long-term rates for reasons which again relate to the enforcement of a personal responsibility. If unemployment and sickness generally are unforeseen contingencies, *long-term* unemployment or sickness involve a predictable set of circumstances to which the individual should adjust; 'there should be room for re-adjustment in such matters as rent or retrenchment in the margin [allowed for wasteful expenditure]' (*SIAS*, p. 87). Beveridge accepted that readjustment and retrenchment was not easy. But he did assume that indefinite benefit at the standard rate represented a concession by the state; and higher standards of personal responsibility were required of those who took advantage of this concession.

Finally, if we consider the question of the relation between benefit levels, we encounter an inflection of the earlier arguments; subsistence adequacy in the state scheme is here compromised in the interests of encouraging an upper tier of voluntary insurance. *SIAS* proposed to pay the same benefit levels in sickness and unemployment. This was administratively straightforward and avoided a situation where there was an incentive to claim one form of benefit rather than another (*SIAS*, p. 54). But, as Beveridge recognised, in subsistence adequacy terms, the standard benefit was also unfair to the sick: 'The sick man needs as a rule more income than the fit unemployed man for special food or for attention; the unemployed man also has more chance of small subsidiary earnings' (*SIAS*, p. 55). However, Beveridge goes on immediately to argue that the need for an adequate benefit in sickness is outweighed by the political need to maintain voluntary insurance: 'On the other hand, voluntary provision to supplement State benefit is both easier to make and much more widely made, for sickness than for unemployment. Equality of benefit is the safest line' (*SIAS*, p. 55).

From the argument so far it may appear that the new social contract between the citizen and the state puts a good deal of responsibility on the individual citizen. And it would be fair to say that Beveridge's liberal collectivist position is defined by this peculiar concern for the maintenance of personal responsibility. But Beveridge was also, at the same time, a radical collectivist who envisaged that the new social contract would make the government responsible for much more than administering a flat-rate insurance scheme. As *SIAS* observed, 'Government should not feel that by paying doles it can avoid the major responsibility of seeing that unemployment and disease are reduced to a minimum' (*SIAS*, p. 12). The success of income maintenance through social insurance depends on a series of external conditions which must be established by positive government action. This is the point which is emphasised by the Beveridge Report's famous corollary assumptions about the state's organisation of a comprehensive National Health Service and the state's 'maintenance of employment'. From our point of view, the latter assumption is the

interesting one and Beveridge himself identifies it as 'the most important of his assumptions' (*SIAS*, p. 154). What exactly did the maintenance of employment require and why did Beveridge consider it to
be the most important of his assumptions?

Beveridge's social insurance scheme represented the limit of what
was financially possible within the constraints of a flat-rate contributory scheme. The insurance fund could only be made to balance
by paying child allowances out of general taxation and by arranging
a twenty-year lead-in to the payment of full old age pensions. With
these decisions taken, unemployment was the remaining impon-
derable which threatened the financial stability of the scheme because
every unemployed person would draw indefinite insurance benefit
without making any contributions to the fund. The fund was balanced
on the assumption that post-war unemployment would average 8.5
per cent amongst manual workers or class 1 contributors (*SIAS*,
pp. 164, 185). If unemployment reached the inter-war level of 10 to
20 per cent large financial deficits would result and the *SIAS* scheme
would also be threatened in other ways. *SIAS* rejected the inter-war
type of insurance scheme which dealt with 'moral hazard' problems
by adopting various restrictive contributory conditions (limits on
benefit duration and tight ratios of benefits to contributions, etc.).
The *SIAS* scheme proposed to abolish contributory conditions and to
curb involuntary unemployment by the offer of a job through the
employment exchange system:

> Men and women in receipt of unemployment benefit cannot be
> allowed to hold out indefinitely for work of the type to which they
> are used, or in their present places of residence, if there is work
> which they could do available at the standard wage for that work.
> (*SIAS*, p. 58)

As Beveridge recognised, this control would only work in conditions
of reasonably full employment.

Less well known, but equally important, is the point that *SIAS*
required more than reasonably full employment; it was equally necessary to abolish long unemployment and to create jobs which paid
decent wages. Beveridge explicitly assumed that long-term unemployment of the same individual for more than twenty-six weeks
'would be reduced to a negligible amount' (*SIAS*, p. 185). This was
necessary not so much because long-term unemployment strained the
fund financially but more because cash benefits were inappropriate
for the long-run unemployed:

> The proposal of this Report ... is to make unemployment benefit
> after a certain point conditional upon attendance at a work or

training centre. But this proposal is impracticable if it has to be applied to men by the million or the hundred thousand. (*SIAS*, p. 163)

A heterogeneous working population would inevitably contain some unemployment-prone individuals who, as Charles Booth said, 'cannot do anything well and ... cannot get up in the morning'. The goal of curbing long-term unemployment was therefore a very ambitious one and it probably required full or over-full employment.

In other ways too, *SIAS* required more than full employment because it assumed that all male workers would be able to obtain full-time jobs at decent standard wages. This assumption was never made explicit but it is implicit in the design of the child allowance scheme which presupposes that male earnings will be sufficient to support a wife and one child. It is also implicit in the whole design of a social insurance scheme for a preponderantly male labour force; the vast majority of married women would not work and they would be provided for as dependent housewives (*SIAS*, p. 89). In the late 1930s, no more than one in seven of married women were in employment and Beveridge envisaged the proportion in work would not be much larger when the war was over; 'the small minority of women who under-take paid employment or other gainful occupation after marriage ... require special treatment' (*SIAS*, p. 50). It was also assumed that the earnings of this small minority would usually be supplementary in a household where there was a male chief wage earner; 'the housewife's earnings in general are a means, not of subsistence, but of a standard of living above subsistence' (*SIAS*, p. 49).

Beveridge was a radical who set the plan for post-war income maintenance very firmly in an economic and social context. *SIAS* does make the connection between social policy and the economic process; secondary income maintenance through social security can only succeed where primary income distribution through the wages system is satisfactory. It was not part of the *SIAS* remit to analyse how decent jobs for all could be obtained. If we wish to analyse the liberal collectivist position on what impedes full employment and how full employment might be obtained, then we must turn to Keynes and the *General Theory*.

The political *a priori* in the *GT*

Because policy recommendations figure much less strongly in the *GT*, the commitment to liberal collectivism is much less obvious than in *SIAS*. But, in a different way, the political *a priori* does feature just as powerfully because Keynes's concern is to provide a theoretical analysis which establishes the necessity for, and vindicates the possibility of, a minimal state intervention which will secure full employment in an otherwise unmodified market system.

To begin with, the necessity for state intervention is established by arguments about the difficulty of controlling unemployment and economic insecurity in a free market economy. According to marginalist theory, if unemployment exists, it should be abolished automatically by a reduction in money wages and therefore production costs which should feed through into a permanent increase in output and employment. As we have noted, where unemployment persists, the marginalist blames organised workers and their trade unions who make money wages sticky. In this case, the problem is not that automatic adjustment mechanisms do not exist, the problem is that they are not being respected and allowed to operate. Keynes's position is that all this is too simple by half and that it is necessary to analyse theoretically the 'roundabout repercussions' of a reduction in money wages which are seldom as straightforwardly beneficial as the marginalist supposes: 'It may well be that the classical theory represents the way in which we should like our Economy to behave. But to assume that it actually does so is to assume our difficulties away' (*GT*, p. 34).

In the *GT* the effect of money wage reductions depends on whether they stimulate or depress consumption and investment expenditures. As these expenditures are determined by the marginal propensity to consume (mpc) and the marginal efficiency of capital (mec), the question is how do wage reductions affect these key independent variables. The mpc exercises a permanently depressing economic influence because it is assumed to be always less than unity. This depressive influence will be reinforced by a reduction in money wages which has a regressive impact on income distribution and thereby tends to reduce rather than increase the mpc. Consequently, the crucial consideration is the impact of a fall in money wages on the mec. The mec depends on business expectations of future yields on capital goods and a fall in money wages in itself has no effect. But business expectations will be affected by judgments of the significance of a given fall in wages relative to future wage levels. There is one (and only one) condition in which a fall in money wages is conducive to an increase in mec: 'The contingency, which is favourable to an increase in the marginal efficiency of capital, is that in which money-wages are believed to have touched bottom, so that further changes are expected to be in the upward direction' (*GT*, p. 265) If this condition is not met, Keynes argues that the marginalist analysis of wage reductions involves a logical fallacy of composition. Wage cuts, at the level of an enterprise or industry, will *ceteris paribus* increase the demand for the products of that enterprise or industry. But wage cuts across the board in the economy as a whole are likely to reduce aggregate effective demand because they will not ordinarily stimulate business expectations and thus the mec so as to compensate for the depressing influence of the mpc. Much must therefore depend on whether the key condition about the business expectation of wages 'touching bottom' can be satisfied. The *GT* maintains that this requires a sudden and dramatic fall in money wages which is not feasible given the existence of free trade unions. Thus Keynes poses a paradox for classical theory. An authoritarian political system is the precondition for 'automatic' adjustment because the dramatic and sudden fall of wages 'could only be accomplished by administrative decree and is scarcely practical politics under a system of free wage bargaining' (*GT*, p. 265). A policy of across the board wage reductions could reduce unemployment, but only if that policy were politically sponsored and pushed through at the expense of the political freedom of the working class and their trade union institutions. Ultimately, therefore, the problem is not that mechanisms of adjustment do not exist or cannot operate. The problem is that these mechanisms can only operate at an unacceptably high political price because they are incompatible with capitalist freedom which includes free collective bargaining.

A more congenial and politically acceptable policy solution is necessary for liberal collectivism. But such a solution is only possible if unemployment in a capitalist market economy is established as a tractable problem which can be dealt with by a minimal state intervention. Keynes's theoretical work in the *GT* must therefore carefully establish that unemployment is amenable to liberal collectivist treatment. It does this by admitting that capitalism can malfunction and produce unemployment while insisting that there is nothing inherently unstable or unsound in the capitalist production process. Both requirements must be met in a kind of intellectual balancing act if the political position is to be sustained and vindicated.

Keynes tries to satisfy the requirements of the *a priori* by locating the causes of unemployment and economic instability in a kind of subjective psychological overlay on top of an objectively sound production process. In the *GT* everything depends theoretically on the stable psychology of consumers and the unstable psychology of investors. Keynes hangs underconsumption on the 'psychological law' (*GT*, p. 27) that the mpc, is always less than one: 'men are disposed, as a rule and on the average, to increase their consumption as their income increases, but not by as much as the increase in their income' (*GT*, p. 96). Keynes hangs the failure of investment expenditure to compensate for this underconsumption equally directly on investor psychology: 'the volume of investment is unplanned and uncontrolled, subject to the vagaries of the marginal efficiency of capital as determined by the private judgement of individuals ignorant or speculative' (*GT*, p. 324).

These psychological propensities are universals which survive despite historical changes in institutional structure and national circumstance: 'there has been a chronic tendency throughout human history for the propensity to save to be stronger than the inducement to invest. The weakness of the inducement to invest has been at all times the key to the economic problem' (*GT*, pp. 347–8). The national economy thus becomes the sphere of interplay of these 'fundamental psychological factors' (mpc and mec) which determine consumption and investment expenditure and hence aggregate effective demand. With the national economy represented in this way, objective circumstances cannot be a problem; nothing except subjective human psychology stands in the way of raising consumption and investment expenditures. And Keynes also assumes, more or less explicitly, that if consumption and investment expenditures are raised the effects on domestic employment and output will always be unequivocally beneficial. It is, for example, assumed without discussion that new investment always creates more employment at standard wages. Keynes in the *GT* never confronts the possibility that expenditure on sophisticated capital equipment might displace part of the existing workforce. Or again, it is assumed after a very brief discussion, that foreign trade will not be a problem as long as all countries simultaneously pursue expansionist policies. Keynes never considers the possibility that an expansion of domestic demand might divert exports or draw in imports because of problems about the pattern of specialisation or problems about uncompetitiveness on cost or quality grounds.

The peculiarity of this emphasis on subjective psychology emerges very clearly if we compare Keynes with earlier and more radically pessimistic theorists of underconsumption and overinvestment such as Marx, Hobson or Gesell. These theorists had attributed the existence and persistence of unemployment to demand deficiency. But this demand deficiency was related to objective structural features of the capitalist production and distribution process; underconsumption is caused by unequal exchange or the maldistribution of wealth, and the failure of investment expenditure is caused by the accumulation of capital or a declining rate of return. From their analysis of objective economic problems, the earlier radical theorists had generally concluded that capitalism was increasingly unstable and suffered from a worsening secular problem of demand deficiency. These earlier radical theories have straightforward political implications. If they are correct, unemployment in the capitalist system is irremediable or can only be modified by a major modification of the system; a minimal state intervention of any kind would be futile. When the political stakes are so high, it is not surprising that the *GT* is concerned at every turn to deny earlier and more radical analyses and conclusions.

We will demonstrate this point by examining the *GT*'s position on accumulation of capital and on the nature of economic instability under capitalism.

On the accumulation of capital, Keynes insists that there is no shortage of useful capital projects: 'The situation, which I am indicating as typical, is not one in which capital is so abundant that the community as a whole has no reasonable use for any more' (*GT*, p. 321). There is equally no problem about obtaining a positive rate of return on useful projects. The *GT* explicitly denies that there is a problem of over-investment 'in the strict sense' with 'every kind of capital good so abundant that there is no new investment which is expected, even in conditions of full employment, to earn in the course of its life more than its replacement cost' (*GT*, p. 321).

Keynes does occasionally hint at secular accumulation problems (e.g. *GT*, pp. 31, 308, 348). But he does not seem to be worried by this prospect partly because he contemplates a world of zero rates of return with equanimity; capitalism would survive in a future world where the aggregate return covered only labour costs of production plus an allowance for risk and the costs of skill and supervision. Indeed, it would be positively beneficial to abolish the 'existing scarcity of capital' which keeps interest rates high and maintains a rentier class of functionless investors (*GT*, p. 376). 'The rentier aspect of capitalism is a transitional phase which will disappear when it has done its work' (*GT*, p. 376). Meanwhile, here and now, the problem about rates of return is a problem about their volatility and this volatility is entirely determined by the psychology of rentiers and businessmen:

> it is an essential characteristic of the boom that investments which will in fact yield, say 2 per cent in conditions of full employment are made in the expectation of a yield of say 6 per cent, and are valued accordingly. When the disillusion comes, this expectation is replaced by a contrary 'error of pessimism' with the result that the investments which would in fact yield 2 per cent in conditions of full employment are expected to yield less than nothing; and the resulting collapse of new investment then leads to a state of unemployment in which the investments which would have yielded 2 per cent in conditions of full employment, in fact yield less than nothing. (*GT*, p. 321)

If fluctuations are caused by volatile and highly subjective expectations, the resulting fluctuations of output and employment are real enough. If Keynes is to maintain a space for liberal collectivist action, the *GT* must therefore go on to deny that capitalism is violently unstable or suffers from worsening secular problems about demand deficiency:

it is an outstanding characteristic of the economic system in which we live that, whilst it is subject to severe fluctuations in respect of output and employment, it is not violently unstable. Indeed it seems capable of remaining in a chronic condition of sub-normal activity for a considerable period without any marked tendency either towards recovery or towards complete collapse. Moreover, the evidence indicates that full, or even approximately full, employment is a rare and short-lived occurrence. (*GT*, pp. 249–50)

This is a rather sanguine reading of the inter-war experience and it is supported by the analysis in chapter 22 which theorises how and why economic fluctuations must take a moderate, well-damped and self-reversing form. The trade cycle occurs when 'a fickle and highly unstable marginal efficiency of capital' meets a 'fairly stable long-term rate of interest' and investment expenditure is switched on and off according to whether the mec is above or below the rate of interest. But, the resulting economic fluctuations do not threaten to destabilise the whole system because the mec does not stay low or high for very long when business expectations change. The bubble of unrealistic expectations bursts at the top of the boom as 'disillusion falls upon an over-optimistic and over-bought market' (*GT*, p. 316). And business pessimism lifts as capital equipment wears out after three to five years and shortage of capital through use causes an obvious scarcity (*GT*, p. 317).

If Keynes is preoccupied with opening up a space for liberal collectivist intervention against unemployment, the *GT* is much less concerned to specify in detail the policies which could fill this space. To some extent, this is inevitable in a work of high theory; the policy implications of such theory are seldom clear cut when the discourse is so rarefied and abstract. Matters are further complicated in the *GT* because Keynes leaves much unspecified and undeveloped. The *GT* takes the national economy as its object and pays little attention to the international economy. It is claimed that expansionist policy 'helps ourselves and our neighbours at the same time' (*GT*, p. 349). But there is no discussion of the institutional arrangements (payments system, etc.) which would be necessary to secure this result. Nor is there any discussion of how disadvantaged and uncompetitive national economies might adjust through say devaluation and price changes under such a system. Even in the domestic context, the aims of Keynesian policy are unclear. The sections on the euthanasia of the rentier suggest that our aim should be to learn to live with a low mec and rate of return. But elsewhere in the *GT* Keynes talks about maintaining a permanent 'quasi-boom' which would presumably be associated with a high mec (*GT*, p. 322).

If much is ambiguous, some things are clear. In general, the task of the policy maker is to 'select those variables which can be deliberately controlled or managed by central authority in the kind of system in which we actually live' (*GT*, p. 247). This requires technical and political forms of calculation. Technically, the problem is to create new policy instruments which are powerful enough to compensate for the general tendency towards unemployment. This point emerges from Keynes's discussion of orthodox monetary policy and the role of interest rate changes. Keynes favours a 'much lower rate of interest' but recognises that cheap money will not be enough when the mec is so volatile and 'errors of pessimism' are powerfully self-fulfilling (*GT*, pp. 247, 330, 378). The introduction of new policy instruments is then subject to a form of political calculation. The *GT* adopts a political position on intervention in the capitalist economy which is classically liberal collectivist. Like Beveridge, Keynes believes in a capitalist market system on the grounds that it secures economic efficiency and safeguards individual freedom (*GT*, p. 379). But capitalism cannot work without some form of collectivist intervention and management; as we have seen, in the *GT* this is because the automatic mechanisms can only work under an authoritarian political regime. In this situation, the liberal collectivist's preferred solution would be some form of intervention which was technically sufficient and minimal so that it would be possible to eliminate unemployment while preserving a 'wide field for the exercise of private initiative and responsibility' (*GT*, p. 379).

The *GT*'s discussion of new policy instruments is dominated by the proposal in chapter 24 for a 'somewhat comprehensive socialisation of investment'. This solution was privileged partly no doubt because it matched his diagnosis of the problem: if the psychology of investors caused the economic problem, then the state could intervene to regulate investment.

> In conditions of laissez-faire the avoidance of wide fluctuations in employment may, therefore, prove impossible without a far-reaching change in the psychology of investment markets such as there is no reason to expect. I conclude that the duty of ordering the current volume of investment cannot safely be left in private hands. (*GT*, p. 320)

If the state should intervene to regulate investment, the *GT* proposed that this should be done in a politically circumspect way so that socialism was avoided.

> It is not the ownership of the instruments of production which it is important for the State to assume. If the State is able to determine the aggregate amount of resources devoted to

augmenting the instruments and the basic rate of reward to those
who own them, it will have accomplished all that is necessary.
(*GT*, p. 378)

This new kind of intervention was defended using classic liberal collectivist arguments. It was a minimal intervention after which 'wide
fields of activity will be unaffected' by government (*GT*, p. 378).
Furthermore, this minimal collectivist intervention was absolutely
necessary if the rest of individualism was to be observed. Socialisation
of investment was 'the only practicable means of avoiding the destruction of existing economic forms in their entirety and ... the condition
of the successful functioning of individual initiative' (*GT*, p. 380).

In many ways, therefore, the socialisation of investment proposal
occupied a political place in Keynesian economics which corresponds
to that of flat-rate social insurance in Beveridge's social scheme.
Ultimately, it does not have quite the same status because socialisation
of investment is not the sole principle of the new economic intervention. In various throwaways, the *GT* suggests that the socialisation
of investment is not enough.

> Whilst aiming at a socially controlled rate of investment with a
> view to a progressive decline in the marginal efficiency of capital,
> I should support at the same time all sorts of policies for increasing
> the propensity to consume. For it is unlikely that full employment
> can be maintained, whatever we may do about investment, with
> the existing propensity to consume. There is room, therefore for
> both policies to operate together. (*GT*, p. 325)

This suggestion is rather confusing because Keynes never specifies
what policies could or should be used to manipulate the mpc. Further
complications are introduced by the famous section at the end of
chapter 10 where Keynes suggests that *any* kind of loan-financed
expenditure by the state would usefully help to stimulate demand.
For this purpose, Keynes notes that the social expenditure could take
a wasteful rather than a useful form. Keynes would clearly prefer the
construction of roads, hospitals and schools but wars, pyramid building and surrealist events like the sponsored recovery of buried bank
notes would have the same effect of stimulating demand (*GT*, p. 128).
Finally, we should also note that Keynes did not recommend but did
tolerantly consider some thoroughly heretical policy proposals like
Gesell's proposals for stamped money (*GT*, p. 355).

Overall, our conclusion must be that the *GT*'s approach to policy was
cheerfully opportunistic. Keynes does not seem to have cared too
much about what was done provided that the policies were technically
adequate and not politically offensive. It is also true that many of the

policies which the *GT* recommended were not very new or exclusively Keynesian. By the late 1930s there was considerable middle-of-the-road academic support for domestic reflation. The unorthodox had been convinced of the benefit of public works long before that. Keynes himself had supported the Liberal proposals for loan-financed road building in 1929, while many Edwardian radicals, like the Webbs or Rowntree, had included counter-cyclical public works as part of a battery of measures to deal with different kinds of unemployment. The *GT* did provide arguments in support of such policies. But many of these arguments had been rehearsed well before 1936. Kahn's 1931 *Economic Journal* article introducing the concept of the multiplier had shown that expenditure on public works had multiplied beneficial effects. But the *GT* did add something. Through its theorisation of the dynamics of the capitalist national economy, the text provided an assurance that policies like loan-financed public works were not only beneficial but also adequate to the situation so that capitalism would survive when these policies were adopted. Unlike *SIAS*, the *GT* did not contribute a distinctive policy to liberal collectivism. More fundamentally the *GT* contributed the concept of a national economic situation where the problems of capitalism were not fundamental and where, consequently, an improvised limited collective intervention against unemployment can succeed.

The limits of liberal collectivism in *SIAS* and the *GT*

So far we have concentrated on an exposition of liberal collectivism in Beveridge and Keynes; a common political strategy can be traced through *SIAS* and the *GT* and the requirements of the *a priori* determine the positions of each of them on many apparently diverse social problems and economic issues. At every point, Beveridge and Keynes are concerned to recommend or justify forms of state intervention which would effectively curb poverty and economic insecurity while preserving as much as possible of the benefits of individual freedom. If there is a field of choice between individualism and collectivism, the Beveridge and Keynes position is an immediately attractive one because it promises to combine the best of both the capitalist and socialist worlds. Partly for this reason the liberal collectivist position has been and is popular. It was first developed in Britain in the 1930s by the more conservative protagonists of planning; Macmillan's text *The Middle Way* (1937) is a classic statement of liberal collectivism. In 1950s Europe, liberal collectivism was restated by the German theorists of the 'social market economy'; Erhard's dictum was 'as much capitalism as possible and as much planning as necessary'. In the 1980s in Britain, the SDP and sections of the Tory party are equally attracted by liberal collectivism, although these ideologues incline much more towards the market than did Beveridge and Keynes. Elsewhere in Europe, from a very different and explicitly socialist position, the French government is moving towards a 'social market' strategy.

But, in this section, we must now question whether it is possible to have the best of both worlds. It is at least arguable that Beveridge and Keynes, like later protagonists of liberal collectivism, refuse to face up to a basic dilemma; either state intervention against poverty and insecurity is much less effective than they wish it to be, or state intervention must be pushed until it threatens the cherished capitalist political and economic freedoms. It is, of course, impossible to demonstrate that this dilemma is a real one in a couple of thousand words. What we can demonstrate is that Beveridge and Keynes unreasonably conjure away this dilemma which otherwise threatens their position. In *SIAS* and the *GT*, the conjuring trick is managed by combining a romantic representation of traditional capitalism with an unrealistic commitment to new forms of collectivism. Beveridge and Keynes romantically overestimate the rationality of the capitalist process; against this, we would argue that the irrational processes and effects of a liberal capitalist economy are much more deep-seated then Beveridge and Keynes want them to be. Equally, Beveridge and Keynes unrealistically underestimate the difficulty of controlled and limited state intervention; against this, we would argue that collectivist intervention cannot be formed, directed and constrained in its effects as Beveridge and Keynes suppose. Our arguments on these points again take Beveridge's and Keynes's own analyses as the point of departure. But in this section we will no longer be demonstrating the existence of a kind of political coherence in *SIAS* and the *GT*; our arguments will now pick up on incoherence in the texts. By shifting the focus of analysis on to awkward corners, loose ends, gaps and judicious silences, we are explicitly leaving behind any kind of problematic of authorial intention. There is no doubt that Beveridge and Keynes intended liberal collectivism to work and sincerely believed it could work. Our thesis now is that their arguments and analyses are unconvincing and there are serious internal problems in *SIAS* and the *GT*. This gives us good reason to doubt whether liberal collectivism can work.

Beveridge's romantic attachment to individualism emerges most strongly in his later text *Voluntary Action*. But there are strong indications of it in the treatment of some important issues in *SIAS*. We will demonstrate this point by considering Beveridge's position on private life insurance.

In inter-war Britain private life insurance was offered in two distinct forms. 'Ordinary life assurance' for the middle classes offered a sizeable lump sum at death to cover the needs of dependants with the option of an endowment if the policy matured before death. 'Industrial life assurance' for the working classes offered a small lump sum at death to cover funeral expenses and avoid a pauper's funeral. Beveridge proposed to make industrial assurance into a 'public service'. If the state paid a £20 grant at death to cover the necessary expenses of a 'decent funeral', the working classes would no longer have a motive to take out industrial assurance (*SIAS*, p. 66). If some of what had been spent on industrial assurance was released, this would incidentally make the high flat-rate contributions of the Beveridge insurance scheme very much more acceptable:

> If only half of what is now devoted to insurance premiums, and only three-quarters of what is now devoted to medical treatment, were regarded as available as contributions to the compulsory insurance scheme, the proposed [manual worker's] contribution of 4s. 3d. [21p] could be met without any difficulty. (*SIAS*, p. 114)

But Beveridge's position on industrial assurance rested on more than arguments of expediency.

To begin with, Beveridge trenchantly criticised the waste which resulted from the selling methods of the industrial assurance companies. An army of collectors on door-to-door rounds collected premiums from the working class at the rate of a few pence weekly or monthly. As a result, the ratio of administrative expenses to premium income was more than twice as high as in ordinary life assurance; 'ordinary life assurance, in spite of growing charges for commission, costs the policy holder not 7s. 6d. [37p] in the pound of premiums but about 3s. 2d. [16p] in the pound' (*SIAS*, p. 261). As is often the case in direct selling, the companies with the more aggressive and expensive selling techniques had increased their market share; responsible companies, like the Prudential and the Refuge, had successfully reduced administrative cost as a percentage of premium and had been rewarded with a slower than average growth of industrial assurance premium income (*SIAS*, p. 258). The most effective way of motivating the collectors was to offer 'procuration fees' on new business and this encouraged them to sell new industrial assurance policies and to condone the lapse of old policies when policy holders did not keep up the premium; a collecting society like the Royal Liver issued 811,000 policies in 1929 and accepted 444,000 lapses (*SIAS*, p. 266).

Interestingly enough, however, the case for intervention in the field of industrial assurance is not based ultimately on the nature of the business practices of the companies. It is the characteristics of the working-class consumer which make a state supervised contract necessary.

> The proposal that the life assurance among persons of limited means should be a public service rather than a competitive private

business is based upon the special character of industrial assurance as a business in which competition leads to over-selling and as a business in which the seller's interests present a danger to the consumer.... Industrial assurance is different from ordinary life assurance, because those who undertake the latter have both, as a rule, less limited means and the possibility of recourse to independent advice. The consumers of industrial assurance have not this recourse: they should be guided in their choice of insurance by advice that is wholly disinterested. (*SIAS*, p. 275)

If intervention is rested in this way on the characteristics of the consumer, there is one crucial implication. Since middle-class saving is undertaken by those who have a substantial margin above subsistence and recourse to independent advice, then it need not be state-managed or regulated. It is simply the sphere of free contract.

The actual incomes and by consequence the normal standards of expenditure of different sections of the population differ greatly. Making provision for these higher standards is primarily the function of the individual, that is to say, it is a matter of free choice and voluntary insurance. (*SIAS*, p. 121)

What follows from this is that the effects of middle-class saving need not be considered; presumably, *caveat emptor* is all that could or should be said about the savings contracts which the middle classes enter into. In fact, Beveridge is completely silent about the effects of middle-class saving.

Beveridge's position on insurance rests on a dichotomy between those in the working classes whose contractual arrangements have to be supervised and those in the middle classes whose contracts should be unregulated because their contracts are a manifestation of capitalist freedom. This position on middle-class saving was romantic. To begin with, Beveridge represented middle-class saving as 'voluntary' when the most important form of middle-class saving was the compulsory superannuation scheme. Such schemes were already commonplace in occupations like the civil service and teaching; one-tenth of retired persons were covered by superannuation schemes by the late 1930s (*SIAS*, p. 92). Furthermore, Beveridge ignored the role of the fiscal system in subsidising various forms of middle-class savings; for example, middle-class taxpayers could already claim tax relief on life insurance premiums before the Second World War. It would be pointless and anachronistic to criticise Beveridge for failing to foresee the massive development of occupational welfare since the Second World War, when occupational pensions, company cars and fiscal privileges for middle-class saving have acted as accelerators of inequality. But we must recognise that Beveridge's romantic position on middle-class saving creates a free space for an upper tier of private welfare which is state-subsidised yet unregulated. Beveridge did not intend this but that is the implication of his position.

Beveridge did intend that the lower collectivist tier of state-provided income maintenance should take the form of a social insurance scheme: 'The scheme of social insurance is designed of itself when in full operation to guarantee the income needed for subsistence in all normal cases' (*SIAS*, p. 12). As we have seen in our examination of the *a priori*, it is politically congenial if state intervention is formed and directed in this way. And it was more or less inevitable that insurance should occupy a prominent place in any early 1940s scheme for the reform of income maintenance. As we have already noted, with the PAYE scheme in its infancy, Beveridge's emphasis on social insurance to some extent simply reflected the limits of what was then technically possible. But it is doubtful whether it was ever realistic to suppose that social insurance could dominate the whole field of income mainten-ance. Strictly speaking, if social insurance was to be dominant, two preconditions would have to be satisfied: first, the social problem would have to present itself in a particular form with short-term dependence as the major problem; and, second, the social insurance fund would have to have a substantial and elastic revenue base so that long-term dependence could be supported. Neither of these conditions could plausibly be satisfied.

SIAS simply fudged these issues by insisting that the social problem was one of 'interruption or loss of earning power' (e.g. *SIAS*, p. 7). Beveridge did not discriminate between or assess the relative size of short- and long-term dependence, let alone estimate how the balance between short- and long-term dependence would shift as the numbers of old persons and unemployed changed over time. *SIAS* recognises these issues only obliquely in its treatment of unemployment. Here, as we have seen, Beveridge commits himself to the optimistic assump-tion of 8.5 per cent post-war unemployment and the implausible assumption that it is possible to abolish long-term unemployment in a heterogeneous population. He also proposed that the scheme should suffer long-term dependence because, as we have noted, the scheme had no contributory conditions which would disqualify the long-term unemployed or sick. But that solution was hardly administratively practical if, as we have argued, the revenue base of the flat-rate insurance scheme was restricted and inelastic. The limits of the rev-enue base, and the difficulty of providing for long-term dependence from that base, were tellingly admitted in Beveridge's own design. In *SIAS*, the insurance fund had to be relieved of all the cost of child allowances and, under the twenty-year lead-in provision, the fund was also relieved of part of the cost of maintaining old age pensioners.

It would be anachronistic to criticise Beveridge for failing to foresee
new patterns of long-term dependence which emerged after 1945; the
rise of divorce and separation alone ensured that there were more
than one million single parents with dependent children in Britain by
the early 1980s. But we must recognise that Beveridge's scheme creates
a space where, in administering insurance, the government will be
constantly tempted to restrict entitlement so as to ease severe financial
constraints. What governments did after 1945 was not so much to
deviate from the Beveridge Plan as to thrash around in the Beveridge
constraints. For example, contributory conditions were introduced as
a back stop on the payment of insurance benefit to the long-term
unemployed; since 1945 it has never been possible to draw unemployment benefit for more than a year. In one important way pensioners were treated more generously than Beveridge had proposed
because full pensions were paid without a twenty-year lead-in. On
the other hand, flat-rate insurance benefits (and child allowances)
were pitched relatively low and tardily adjusted to take account of
inflation. As a result, assistance acquired a relatively large role in
topping up basic insurance benefits. One way or another, a relatively
large role for assistance was inevitable; post-war governments only
chose how assistance was used to supplement an insurance fund which
could not meet all the calls on it.

What *SIAS* had not thought through, and could not confront, was
the issue of what would happen when the role of assistance (one
way or another) turned out to be larger and more permanent than
Beveridge had intended. The basic design of assistance was subordinated to the requirements of the more politically congenial
insurance scheme. Crucially, there had to be a means test for assistance
benefits so as to encourage insurance contributors whose benefits
would not be means tested:

> assistance will be available to meet all needs which are not covered
> by insurance. It must meet those needs adequately up to
> subsistence level, but it must be felt to be something less desirable
> than insurance benefit; otherwise the insured persons get nothing
> for their contributions. Assistance, therefore, will be given always
> subject to proof of means and examination of needs. (*SIAS*, p. 141)

Society would have to suffer the consequences. As we have already
noted, Beveridge himself believed that means tests discouraged thrift
and saving. More to the point, subsequent experience had shown that
means tests always led to problems about take-up of benefit, either
because claimants do not know what or how to claim or because
claimants are unwilling to claim. Beveridge never intended to create
a maintenance system where means tests were a major feature and low

take-up rates were a massive problem. But that was the implication of his unreasonable view that one politically congenial principle could cover the whole field of social needs in income maintenance.

A similar mix of romance and unreality can be found if we examine Keynes's *GT*. Here, the romantic attachment to individualism is mediated through theory. This emerges very clearly if we examine Keynes's position on marginalism as a theory of how the market economy should work and as the putative principle underlying the real allocation of resources in such an economy. It is well known that orthodox economic discourse annexed Keynes's *GT* as a matter of supplementary insight and complementary theoretical structure; the widespread acceptance of this view is reflected in the organisation of the average post-war economics textbook with its marginalist macro front half and its Keynesian macro back half. Keynes himself prepared the way for this reconciliation by (mis)representing his relation to marginalism.

After destroying the marginalist explanation of unemployment, Keynes tries hard to preserve what remains of the marginalist theory of production and distribution. Chapter 1 sets up a crucial opposition between 'general theory' and 'special case' (*GT*, p. 3). This opposition is crucial to how Keynes thinks his novelty and represents his relation to marginalism. Marginalism is entirely unable to provide a 'general theory' of output and employment. As its title indicates, the *GT* is designed to redress this absence. But, in the 'special case' of full employment, marginalism can provide a 'theory of [production by] the individual firm and of the distribution of the product resulting from the employment of a given quantity of resources' (*GT*, p. 340). In this respect, classical theory is a 'contribution to economic thinking which cannot be impugned' (*GT*, p. 340). Keynes tries to limit his criticism of marginalism by insisting that marginalism is valid once full employment is reached and also for some micro parts of the economy. The implication is that, if marginalism is respected, the market could also provide the basis for a rational and efficient alloca-tion of resources, at least when the economy is at or near full employ-ment. Meanwhile Keynes is reasonably complacent that, away from full employment, such an allocation of resources already does exist. There is no suspicion that the existing system seriously misemploys the factors of production which are in use; the problem is not that nine million men 'ought to be employed on different tasks but that tasks should be available for the remaining one million men' (*GT*, p. 379).

There is one problem with all this. The supposed relation between the two bodies of theory and the presumed real allocative result are both entirely incompatible with Keynes's own account of the investment decision. The marginal efficiency of capital is a new con-cept which preserves the word marginal rather than the substance of marginalism. As chapter 5 makes clear, new investment is determined by 'expectations of results' from new investment rather than by any 'realised results' at the margin (*GT*, p. 47). These expectations are not rational. Any form of investment calculation will be confused by 'speculation' and attempts to outguess 'the psychology of the market' (*GT*, p. 155). Even if such speculation were removed, according to the *GT*, the investment decision is necessarily 'ignorant' because it depends on expectations about future returns and there is no rational basis for predicting such returns. Hence Keynes emphasises 'animal spirits' and the way in which 'a large proportion of our positive activities depend on a spontaneous optimism rather than on a mathematical expectation' (*GT*, p. 161). On Keynes's own account of the investment decision, the prevailing forms of enterprise calculation in capitalist economies do not conform to the marginalist model where current yield at the margin should rationally determine every adjustment. The general theory and special case opposition is therefore a misrepresentation which conceals incommensurability and a radical difference of explanatory principle in the *GT*. Furthermore, if the forms of calculation undertaken by enterprises in making new investment do not conform to the marginalist model, then the felicific allocative result can hardly be guaranteed. If speculation and ignorance predominates in the investment decision, then any free market economy must be marred by irrational processes and effects which undermine allocative efficiency.

There is therefore a discrepancy between the radical novelty of the *GT* and how Keynes thinks (or more exactly denies) the novelty of that text. And these denials serve the cause of romantic fiction. Keynes denies the implications of his own theory so as to maintain an idealised view of the market economy. In another register of liberal collectivism, as we have seen, Beveridge clings to an idealised individualism about saving despite all evidence to the contrary. The parallel can be developed further because Keynes's commitment to collectivism was quite as unrealistic as Beveridge's ever was. In the *GT*, as in *SIAS*, there is the problem of whether state intervention can be directed and limited. This point emerges very clearly if we examine the *GT*'s major policy proposal for socialisation of investment.

In various passages, Keynes supposes that the socialisation of investment policy will be used intermittently to provide occasional counter-cyclical nudges when the economy is away from full employment. This is politically congenial because it suggests a limited intervention against the market will be possible; if state-sponsored investment is used to get to full employment, then market allocation by price will rule once full employment is achieved. In a blurred way, this position on the real economy is implicit in a famous passage on the adequacy of classical theory:

the classical theory comes into its own again from this point onwards. If we suppose the volume of output to be given, i.e. to be determined by forces outside the classical scheme of thought, then there is no objection to be raised against the classical analysis of the manner in which private self-interest will determine what in particular is produced, in what proportions the factors of production will be combined to produce it, and how the value of the final product will be distributed between them. (*GT*, p. 378)

Keynes tries to solve the problem of a contradiction between two allocative principles (state regulation of investment v. market allocation of resources) by supposing that they can each be determinant at different moments.

But this is really wishful thinking for a variety of reasons. To begin with, it is clear that intervention cannot be intermittent if the economic system has a chronic tendency to come to rest away from full employment. Keynesian theory established that the system does have this tendency because the mpc is less than one and the mec ensures that investment expenditure does not usually compensate. Aggregate demand will be chronically deficient and, as we have noted, at various points in the argument the *GT* accepts that continuous intervention on several fronts is required to raise investment and consumption expenditure. Even if we suppose that state intervention can be kept intermittent and confined to the regulation of investment, that still creates many problems for a liberal collectivist. This limited intervention is sufficient to threaten the economic efficiency and capitalist political freedoms which Keynes holds so dear.

On allocative efficiency, the question is whether the state's forms of calculation about investment can or will conform to the marginalist model where current yield at the margin should be decisive. In a sense, this question is unreal because, as we have seen, in Keynesian theory enterprises are unable to make exemplary calculations of this sort. But, even if enterprises did calculate in this way, their calculations would hardly determine the allocation of resources if the state was intermittently intervening to regulate investment on different principles. The conditions of allocative efficiency can hardly be satisfied if allocation by price and cost operates within a given framework where the disposition of capital equipment is determined by the state according to different criteria. This issue of criteria cannot be avoided because, if the state is regulating the volume of investment, it will be difficult to avoid state decisions about the priority of different kinds of projects; if a large quantity of investment funds are mobilised for counter-cyclical purposes they will surely have to be directed somewhere. Keynes gives no reason to suppose that the state's investment funds will be disposed according to calculations of current yield at the margin. Indeed, the *GT* emphasises that state investment decisions should 'calculate the marginal efficiency of capital on long views and on the basis of the general social advantage' (*GT*, p. 164). This seems to suggest that the state should not be much preoccupied with current private rates of return.

There is really little prospect of a limited intervention which leaves most market mechanisms economically intact. Furthermore, the political price of effective intervention is also likely to be much higher than Keynes is prepared to admit. At this point it is useful to recall Keynes's objection to the orthodox policy of money wage reductions. As we have seen, Keynes ultimately rejected this policy not because it would never work, but because it was politically incompatible with a system of free, collective bargaining. If a policy of money wage reductions were carried through, its price would be a necessary abridgment of the political freedom of the working class and their trade union institutions. But, in proposing the socialisation of investment, Keynes ironically recommends an alternative policy which is equally problematic from the point of view of maintaining capitalist political freedoms. If state regulation of investment were carried through, it would abridge the economic freedom of the capitalist class and their city institutions. The logic of this seems inescapable when in at least one passage Keynes envisages that the state would determine not only the amount of investment, but also the rate of return; the rentier/investor in this case would become a holder of state coupons. The investors and investing institutions would, in these circumstances, surely resist in the 'traditional' ways using capital flight and a refusal to take up state loans (a 'gilts strike') so that the capitalist class would have to be coerced. Keynes's failure to confront these political implications makes his collectivism quite unreal.

It is appropriate to end with this point about the political price of economic intervention, because it highlights so clearly the tension between the liberal political *a priori* and the problem definitions and policy recommendations in Beveridge or Keynes. They attempt to subordinate these problem definitions and policy recommendations to the requirements of the *a priori*, but ultimately Beveridge and Keynes do not succeed. If they delude themselves about this point, it is because Beveridge and Keynes had a fervid commitment to capitalist economic and political freedom which often gets the better of their sober empirical analysis and theoretical construction. The freedoms of capitalism often turn out to be much more illusory and mixed in their results than these romantics admit or, alternatively, really valuable freedoms are more fundamentally threatened than these unreal collectivists admit. For this reason, the liberal collectivist position which promises the best of both worlds is ultimately a Utopian dream.

2 'Private saving' versus company pensions

In chapter 1 we showed that Beveridge's design for a state system of income maintenance was in many ways determined by the need to 'create a space' for private saving and insurance. In this chapter, we turn to Beveridge's analysis of private saving. The object is to show that there is a discrepancy between the idealised version of private saving which Beveridge approved of, and the reality of what actually existed in 1945 and continues to exist four decades later. The implication is that the whole liberal collectivist demarcation of a proper line of division between the state and private sectors rests on an illusion.

Beveridge is remembered as the author of a state social insurance scheme. It is thus not surprising that we have to reconstruct Beveridge's position on the private sector from two texts which have been virtually ignored and are now entirely unread. The first key text is a neglected section of *Social Insurance and Allied Services* (Appendix D on Industrial Assurance) which deals with the future of private life insurance for the working class. Beveridge regarded this topic as sufficiently important to merit lengthy, detailed and closely argued analysis. The second key text is *Voluntary Action* (1948) which is preoccupied with the prospects of the friendly societies which had long organised private health insurance for lower-income groups. Beveridge presented *Voluntary Action* (1948, pp. 11, 322) quite explicitly as the third in a series of reports which had begun in the 1942 official report on social insurance and been continued with the 1944 unofficial report on full employment. We believe that a consideration of these two key texts will enhance our understanding of Beveridge and of the limits of liberal collectivism.

If Beveridge was a liberal collectivist who believed in a new kind of minimal state intervention, he was never an apologist or enthusiast for market freedom in the private sector. In fact, Beveridge had a Manichaean view of capitalism; the observed mixture of good and evil within the capitalist universe was explained in terms of the opposite agencies of two co-external and independent principles which Beveridge called the motives of 'altruism' and 'selfishness'. In a moralistic and quasi-religious way, capitalism was the sphere of conflict between these motives. In his third report Beveridge was primarily concerned with altruism or 'private enterprise, not in business but in the service of mankind, not for gain but under the driving power of social conscience' (Beveridge, 1948, p. 322). Beveridge supposed that altruism took two characteristic class forms – 'philanthropy' in the middle classes and 'mutual aid' in the working classes. In the field of private saving, the motive of altruism found expression and institutional embodiment in the provision of sickness insurance by friendly societies. Private saving through such institutions reflected 'a sense of one's own need for security against misfortune, and realization that since one's fellows have the same need, by undertaking to help one another, all may help themselves' (Beveridge, 1948, p. 9).

The higher motives of altruism were everywhere challenged by the lower motives of selfishness which were certainly entrenched in the field of private saving. In this field, the first selfish motive was 'personal thrift' or 'saving to have money at one's own command, saving for personal independence' (Beveridge, 1948, p. 9), and the second selfish motive was the 'business motive' or 'the pursuit of a livelihood or of gain for oneself in meeting the needs of one's fellow citizens' (Beveridge, 1948, p. 10). These two motives found expressions in the provision of life insurance for the working class by 'industrial assurance' companies. Here 'the business motive has become dominant, and gain without limit has been sought by doing the simplest possible service' (Beveridge, 1948, p. 8).

Beveridge simultaneously admitted and deprecated the success of the lower motives in the field of personal saving because 'the business motive is a good servant but a bad master, and a society which gives itself up to the dominance of the business motive is a bad society' (Beveridge, 1948, p. 322). However desirable altruism was, it could not be directly created or controlled by the state. Any well-intentioned efforts on these lines would only produce a 'totalitarian society'. But the success of the motive of altruism could be encouraged in a variety of ways by resourceful social engineering. Thus, for example, state intervention could be extended so that the business motive was suppressed and evicted from spheres of private saving where this motive had established itself to the detriment of the consumer. This was the rationale behind Beveridge's proposal for the nationalisation of working-class life insurance in Appendix D of *Social Insurance and the Allied Services*.

When Beveridge was concerned to protect the higher motives, he did not think it at all paradoxical to propose that the state pay a death benefit within the framework of a compulsory state social insurance scheme. This would supplant the industrial assurance companies which had prospered in the business of offering life insurance which covered burial expenses and thus allowed the working class to escape the indignity of a pauper's funeral. This specific type of life insurance had three defining characteristics: (a) it was predominantly used by lower-income groups; (b) premiums were paid frequently, usually weekly; and (c) they were paid to collectors who made home visits. The strategic importance of this form of private saving can be established with one simple statistical comparison. In the late 1930s, private insurance premiums (which according to Beveridge were 'largely payments for industrial assurance') cost the industrial classes more than payments for compulsory state insurance against sickness and unemployment and old age. Private insurance premiums took 28.5 pence per household while the state's social insurance contribution cost just 24.75 pence per household at 1937–8 prices (Beveridge, 1942, hereafter *SIAS*, p. 115). Like other inter-war critics of industrial assurance (e.g. Cohen, 1934; Wilson and Levy, 1937), Beveridge argued that such industrial assurance was poor value for money. This form of private insurance burdened the poor saver with large and unnecessary administrative costs. And a substantial proportion of industrial assurance policies lapsed so that life cover was not effectively maintained. Beveridge followed through the logic of this critique to argue that the dominant form of working-class saving should, in effect, be socialised.

On the question of administrative cost, the pertinent comparison was that between working-class industrial assurance and the 'ordinary' life insurance taken out by middle-class individuals. Industrial assurance came out badly: 'ordinary life assurance, in spite of growing charges for commission, costs the policy holder not 7/6d (37p.) in the pound of premiums but about 3/2d (16p) in the pound' (*SIAS*, p. 261). The problem of lapses had originally been highlighted in Gladstone's famous speech against industrial assurance in the House of Commons in 1864. This remained a significant problem in the later 1930s when barely one-third of industrial assurance policies resulted in claims and payment of benefit. Beveridge gave figures for 'six large offices' for the years 1929, 1937, 1938 and 1939; his table showed that the best figure for percentage of industrial assurance policies reaching maturity was 35.7 per cent (*SIAS*, p. 265).

The nature of the industrial assurance market was such that the undesirable features of this type of life insurance were encouraged rather than corrected. Expenses were high because an army of collectors was employed to collect premiums; approximately 65,000 full-time agents were employed in industrial assurance in 1939 (*SIAS*, p. 250). *Ceteris paribus*, a business which used collectors would have higher administrative costs than one, such as 'ordinary life assurance', which did not; the same product could only be provided at higher cost for the working class. But weekly collection was an inescapable part of this private market because it was the only effective way of collecting premiums from those on low incomes. The problem of lapses was caused by 'over-selling' to this same group. As Wilson and Levy (1937) saw, life insurance was being foisted on to a group whose incomes left little or no margin for regular saving. When the immediate pressure of the hard sell was released, the regular burden of the weekly payment had to be faced and the policy often lapsed. Insofar as agents were paid in the form of commission on new business, there was even an incentive to allow one policy to lapse before returning, after a decent interval, to sell another.

Given the problem about expense ratios, one might at least hope that, over time, the market would select the most efficient insurance organisations with the lowest expense ratios. But the perverse market in working-class life insurance rewarded the organisations with higher expense ratios. In a business where the emphasis was on hard selling by the agent, this was regrettable but not perhaps entirely surprising. In the inter-war period, the so-called 'collecting societies' increased their premium income on this class of business faster than the more responsible and efficient 'proprietary companies' who successfully reduced their expense ratios. The collecting societies succeeded because their salesmen/agents tried harder when they were motivated by the payment of 'extravagant rates of commission' (Cohen, 1934). Furthermore these rates tended to become 'frozen' by the operation of 'book interest'. Under this system, when an agent retired he could nominate his successor who would buy his insurance 'book'. The value of the book was a multiple of weekly premium income and a key determinant of the multiple was the commission rate. Consequently any cut in commission rates would not only reduce the agent's income but also involve him in a capital loss.

It was not difficult to make out a commonsense case for the abolition of a private business which had adapted pathologically to the difficulty of selling any form of life insurance to those on low and irregular incomes. Beveridge was, however, characteristically concerned also to set the case for abolition of industrial assurance in a liberal collectivist problematic. Within such a problematic, there was a need to justify intervention in a sphere of free private contract and interference with the individual's capitalist freedom to do what he wills with his own. By way of justification, Beveridge used two basic arguments about industrial assurance. First, insurance against the expense of a decent funeral was a basic necessity. A state death benefit to cover this expense was a natural part of the universal minimum which state insurance should provide. Second, the characteristics of the working-class consumer of insurance and the relation of that consumer to the product and to the agent who sold insurance was such as to justify intervention which would be inappropriate in the case of the middle-class consumer of 'ordinary life insurance'.

> [Life Assurance] is not an article in regard to which the buyer can, without loss, change his purchase or his seller, if he is dissatisfied. He cannot, having bought insurance from one company one day buy less insurance or different insurance another day ... [Life Assurance] is also an article of whose value in relation to other things it is difficult for the buyer to judge. It is important, therefore, that in buying life assurance persons of limited means should be guided by advice from the seller which is wholly disinterested. This does not apply to life assurance by people who have larger means and in general can have recourse to skilled, disinterested advice. (*SIAS*, p. 75)

From this point of view, it was appropriate to propose a regime of state tutelage for the working-class consumer of insurance who required protection from dishonest advice in a situation where he could not make an informed *ex ante* judgment or easily modify *ex post* a contract which he had entered into. At least two of the three conditions justifying tutelage do not apply to the informed middle-class consumer who has access to financial advisors and other intermediaries. Under the rule of '*caveat emptor*', middle-class individuals should retain the freedom to enter life insurance contracts offered by private companies.

These kinds of argument about the circumstances under which tutelage and the abridgment of free contract is justified can be found in other liberal collectivist texts. Beveridge's proposals and arguments for the partial nationalisation of life insurance are paralleled, for example, by Macmillan's (1937) proposals for the partial national-isation of the production and distribution of consumer goods. In *The Middle Way*, Beveridge-type arguments underpinned Macmillan's proposal that production and distribution of basic goods should be undertaken by the state while the production and distribution of fur coats, gramophones and slim volumes of poetry was to remain in the private sector. This kind of proposal for a solution is politically and aesthetically satisfying for the liberal collectivist but it usually raises almost as many problems as it pretends to solve. This is certainly so in the Beveridge case of life insurance. Here the liberal collectivist rationale for limiting intervention is fundamentally unsound because it rests on a concept of the idealised middle-class consumer which is a gross oversimplification; as we will argue later in this chapter, the dominant forms of private saving do not represent free contracts which are entirely in the private sector. But, for the moment, we wish to raise a more immediate and obvious problem which is created by Beveridge's highly individual fusion of liberal collectivism with an idiosyncratic Manichaean moral view of capitalism: the motives for private saving in the sphere of free contract were obviously 'selfish', so how and why could Beveridge believe that the result would be a morally tolerable society?

Beveridge could not approve of a world where business institutions dominated the provision of services to private savers. In *Voluntary Action* he was quite explicit that 'it would be a pity if the whole field of security against misfortune ... became divided between the State and private business conducted for gain' (Beveridge, 1948, p. 294). This quotation signals the way in which Beveridge by 1948 had gone beyond a classic liberal collectivism which sets up a polar opposition between the state and the market at the same time as it introduces a master problem about where the line between the state and the market should be drawn. The message of his third report in 1948 was that it was unnecessary to choose between the state or the market because voluntary action could and did function as a kind of buffer zone between them. The institutions of voluntary action were not part of the state apparatus; indeed a non-totalitarian society was partly defined by the existence of voluntary associations (like trade unions or co-operative societies) which were not state-controlled (Beveridge, 1948, pp. 8–10). Equally voluntary associations were not part of the market because the altruistic motives of mutual aid and philanthropy sustained them. The scope for voluntary associations with these motives was not diminished in a welfare state with comprehensive social security and full employment because 'the state cannot see to the rendering of all the services that are needed to make a good society' (Beveridge, 1948, p. 304). Under a new division of responsibility in the welfare state, the state would redistribute income while voluntary action provided a range of services, including financial services for savers. In this corner of the field of voluntary action Beveridge emphasised the role which friendly societies could and did play by offering mutual insurance against sickness on a non-profit-making basis.

Beveridge was able to convince himself that, through the agency of friendly societies, popular participation and mass savings were ready to be mobilised under the banner of altruism. But most of the evidence which he himself presented in *Voluntary Action* flatly contradicted this interpretation. This evidence on the current role, historical development and future prospects of friendly societies showed that Beveridge had politically and economically idealised the friendly society movement.

The field of private savings was dominated by other institutions; official statistics published by the registrar of friendly societies showed that building societies and trustee savings banks had mobilised the largest funds. Within the lower income groups, saving through industrial assurance was much more important than saving through friendly societies: in the 1937–40 period, for example, the average annual premium income of the industrial assurance business exceeded the accumulated funds of the affiliated-order type of friendly society. If all of the dominant savings institutions represented the principle of personal thrift, it was also clear that the friendly society movement no longer represented the principle of mutual aid. They had eight million members but effective participation rates were very low; a Research Services survey commissioned by Beveridge showed that seven out of eight friendly society members never attended a meeting at all and practically all attendances were drawn from the older age groups (Beveridge, 1948, pp. 292–3). Beveridge was forced to conclude that, for most of their eight million members, 'the friendly societies today represent not good fellowship but a means of insurance contract' (Beveridge, 1948, p. 293).

This outcome was partly the result of the recent history of the friendly society movement. Beveridge idealised the affiliated-order type of friendly society which maintained 'good fellowship in spite of growth' (Beveridge, 1948, p. 137), but, since 1914, the growth in friendly society membership and in financial resources had been entirely concentrated in the so-called Holloway and Deposit types of friendly society which were geared to individual saving because in these types of friendly society 'the investment interest earned was used to increase the member's individual surplus or deficit' (Beveridge, 1948, p. 329). Beveridge had to admit that the newer types of friendly society appealed to 'the motive of individual saving for emergencies' (Beveridge, 1948, p. 81) and the most successful Holloway societies were models of 'enterprising business' (Beveridge, 1948, p. 51). Just like the hugely successful Post Office Savings Bank, or the more recent national savings movement, these types of friendly society were 'exploiting the purely individual motive' (Beveridge, 1948, p. 69).

A subtler but equally damaging discrepancy between ideal and reality arose over the relation between the friendly society movement as a whole and the state. Friendly societies were not independent institutions of voluntary action. As 'approved societies' in the inter-war period they had functioned as an appendage of state social insurance. Their whole future was called into question when the government decided (against Beveridge's recommendation) that friendly societies would have no role in the post-war administration of sickness insurance. At this turning-point, as Beveridge recognised, the future of friendly societies and of other 'mutual aid' agencies depended on the Treasury's tax regime. Tax concessions were crucial when individual income tax payers paid at a standard rate of 10 shillings (50p) in the pound and surtax payers at a rate of 17 shillings and 6 pence (87p) in the pound.

> Problems of taxation or tax exemption arise in relation not only to
> charitable endowments and philanthropic agencies but also in
> relation to mutual aid agencies of many kinds: friendly societies,
> trade unions, building societies, housing associations and others.
> (Beveridge, 1948, p. 312)

The friendly society goose was cooked when the movement did not
obtain a regime of suitable tax concessions and other institutions of
personal thrift (for example, building societies) obtained or con-
solidated important tax concessions.

Rather endearingly, despite all the evidence to the contrary, Beveridge remained optimistic about the future of friendly societies and of
mutual aid.

> The degree to which the friendly societies triumph over their
> difficulties will depend on their life and the spirit of service in
> them, on their being ready to meet new needs by new methods, in
> the old spirit of social advance by brotherly co-operation. That
> most of them will do so can be taken for certain. The greatest
> danger of the present situation is not on the side of the friendly
> societies. They will survive; if they did not do so, their place would
> be taken by new forms of voluntary organisation. (Beveridge,
> 1948, pp. 83–4)

Beveridge subscribed to a kind of romantic essentialism about voluntary action for mutual purposes. However much contrary evidence
he reviewed, he could not accept that the conception of private welfare
through mutuality among the lower-income groups was a delusion.

The story since 1945 is a simple one. Other 'selfish' forms of private
saving expanded to fill the space which, in Beveridge's fantasy, was
to be occupied by altruistic mutuality. Of all the forms of saving which
flourished outside the state's control, the largest and fastest-growing
was occupational pensions. In 1936 occupational pension scheme
membership stood at just over 2.5 million. In the post-war period,
membership grew substantially; as Table 2.1 shows, it peaked at 12.2
million in 1967. Since then membership has dropped, but around half
the workforce has consistently been found to be scheme members; the
1979 survey of occupational pension schemes by the government
actuary's department revealed that 51 per cent of employees were
members of occupational schemes. This is a big business because
contributions to pension schemes account for a significant part of the
current salaries of the half of the population who are enrolled in
occupational schemes. The annual survey of pension schemes by the
National Association of Pension Funds showed that, in 1983, combined employer and employee contributions amounted to an average

Table 2.1 Employees in pension schemes 1953–1983

Year	Private sector Men	Women	Public sector Men	Women	Total members	Total employed	Percentage of members
1953	2.5	0.6	2.4	0.7	6.2	21.9	28
1956	3.5	0.8	2.9	0.8	8.0	22.7	35
1963	6.4	0.8	3.0	0.9	11.1	22.9	48
1967	6.8	1.3	3.1	1.0	12.2	23.2	53
1971	5.5	1.3	3.2	1.1	11.1	22.5	49
1975	4.9	1.1	3.7	1.7	11.4	23.1	49
1979	4.6	1.5	3.7	1.8	11.6	23.2	50
1983	4.4	1.4	3.4	1.9	11.1	21.1	52

Note: The table now excludes employees who have some pension rights from their current job, but are not currently accruing benefits.
Source: Employment Gazette, December 1985

15 per cent of 'salary' (Government Actuary's Department, 1981, Table 2.1, p. 5; National Association of Pension Funds, 1984). This last statistic cannot be entirely precise because schemes vary in the way in which they define salary.

The relative importance of pension scheme saving is best gauged by comparing the value of employer and employee contributions to pension schemes, which cover half the working population, with the value of employer and employee contributions to national insurance, which covers the whole working population. In 1983 employers' and employees' combined contributions to occupational pension schemes amounted to £16,579 m. (CSO, 1984). This was only marginally below the 1982–3 figure for contributions to the national insurance fund at £16,664 m. (CSO Annual Abstract, 1985). This contrast is the more striking if we remember that contributions to the national insurance fund support the funding, not merely of state retirement pensions, but of the whole range of other insurance benefits including sickness and unemployment benefits. Since state retirement pensions are financed on a 'pay as you go' basis (current expenditure determines contribution rates), it may also be pertinent to compare the figure for private pension contributions with current expenditure on state retirement pensions. In 1982–3 state pensions for all over retirement age cost £13,845 m. (CSO Annual Abstract, 1985) and this was roughly four-fifths (83 per cent) of the current combined contributions to occupational schemes.

A liberal collectivist might argue that the development of occupational pensions on such a scale should be welcomed as a healthy manifestation of the development in new forms of the old capitalist freedom of the individual to do what he wills with his own. This argument is unsustainable however because, as we will now argue, occupational pensions do not represent free contracts which are entirely in the private sector. To begin with, private pension contracts are compulsory. According to the 1983 NAPF Survey, 84 per cent of occupational schemes were compulsory and 93 per cent of members were enrolled in such schemes. Furthermore, these compulsory pension schemes can hardly be considered as private arrangements when a significant proportion of schemes cover public employees and all the private pension schemes are massively subvented by a variety of tax concessions.

It is a paradox of the development of occupational schemes that coverage has been much more extensive for public as against private sector employees. For example, in December 1985 the *Employment Gazette* published data on pension scheme membership in 1983. This showed that while only 52 per cent of private sector male employees were pension scheme members, male membership in the public sector was virtually universal at 94 per cent. Membership amongst women was, as one would expect, lower overall but again was significantly higher in the public sector, 59 per cent of public sector female employees were scheme members as against 24 per cent of private sector female employees (*Employment Gazette*, December 1985, Table 2). The contrast, in the case of women, is even more striking if the comparison is limited to full-time employees. In the public sector membership was virtually universal for full-time female employees at 95 per cent (*ibid.*, Table 3). It is thus a major irony that the real 'flourishing' of occupational pension scheme membership has been in provision for public sector employees.

The tax subventions on occupational pensions are so important that it is worth detailing the nature of the subventions and outlining what they are worth in total. Employer's contributions to occupational pension schemes are deductible as a labour cost for tax purposes. Since this follows general rules about legitimate expenses which can be deducted before the computation of business profits, this is not generally regarded as a tax concession to the employer (Willis and Hardwick, 1978, pp. 29–30). The provisions with regard to the taxation of employees on pension contributions must however be regarded as concessions. The employee's contribution to an 'exempt approved' occupational scheme is deducted from taxable income, that is, the employee pays no tax on this portion of his income because it is not treated as taxable income. The same procedure is adopted with regard to the employer's contribution which is again not treated as part of the individual's taxable income. The Inland Revenue allows tax exempt deductions for employer and employee contributions up to a ceiling of 15 per cent of salary. As a result, occupational pensions are differentiated from other non-wage benefits. For example, even though the benefit is subject to considerable undervaluation, recipients of company cars are obliged to add a figure to taxable pay in respect of this benefit. Pensions are different because no addition is made to taxable pay in respect of the employee's and employer's current contributions which offer the prospect of substantial benefit when the individual retires. Furthermore, the tax concessions do not end at the moment when employee and employer make a contribution; substantial tax concessions are made in respect of the funds accumulating in occupational pension schemes and also when the scheme member finally draws his or her pension. Occupational schemes are usually 'funded', that is to say, contribution income is invested so that a 'fund' is built up and liabilities of the scheme in the form of pension payments are met out of that fund. The investment income of the fund in the form of interest and dividend payments on the securities held is untaxed while capital gains on securities or assets sold are exempt from capital gains tax. Pension receivers benefit equally from the provision that up to one and a half times final remuneration may be 'commuted', that is, taken as a tax free lump sum payment.

It is not easy to quantify the benefits for scheme members and the costs for non-scheme members which are created by the panoply of tax concessions on occupational pensions. Some of the costs for non-scheme members are hidden. For instance, non-scheme members pay additional tax by virtue of the narrowing of the tax base which results from tax concessions to scheme members and their pension funds. The simplest calculations of the value of the benefit to scheme members adds up the value of the different tax concessions which we have outlined. The value of each concession is taken to be the cost to the exchequer of each concession in terms of tax yield foregone. The Inland Revenue gives costings for 1983–4 (Board of Inland Revenue, 1983, p. 2) on this basis:

	£ billion
Tax relief for employees' contributions	1.1
Tax relief for employees' in respect of employers' contributions	1.1
Exemption of pension funds' investment income (assuming tax at 30 per cent and *excluding* capital gains)	2.25
Lump sum exception	£650 million

Simple addition gives a total of £5.1 billion as the official gross value of the tax benefit. From this gross total we should net out the tax yield from pensions in payment at £1.85 billion which leaves £3.25 billion as the official net value of the tax benefit. The tax yield from pensions in payment can be expected to increase as pension funds come to maturity and hence the 1983–4 net cost figure of £3.25 billion might be expected to fall in future. On the other hand it will be noted that the official net £3.25 billion does not include a figure for the value of capital gains exemption which is a major concession. Reddin (Reddin and Pilch, 1985, p. 24) cites an unofficial estimate of the value of this concession and suggests it cost the Treasury an annual average of £1.25 billion over the 1977–80 period. Adding this unofficial estimate of the value of capital gains tax exemption for 1977–80 to the official estimate of the value of the other concessions in 1983 gives a final net figure of £4.5 billion which is both the value of the benefits to the scheme members and the cost of them to the exchequer. From this last point of view it is instructive to compare the £4.5 billion cost of the exchequer's subvention of private pensions with the £2.6 billion cost of the direct exchequer supplement (or subsidy) to the national insurance fund which was only 60 per cent of the 'tax expenditure' figure.

It should also be emphasised that the tax subsidy to occupational pensions is not a special case, because many of the other forms of private saving have been and are tax-subvented and to that extent dependent on the state. One of the great weaknesses of Beveridge's position on 'private saving' was that he never recognised this elementary point or, more exactly, although he accepted the fact of tax subvention, he would not see that it had devastating implications for a liberal collectivism which departed from the assumption of a distinct private sphere. Consider, for example, the case of ordinary life assurance which Beveridge always presented as the model of a private arrangement. Some form of tax relief on life assurance premiums has applied throughout the whole period since the introduction of income tax in 1799, with the exception of the period 1842–53 (Millard Tucker, 1954, pp. 5–9; Willis and Hardwick, 1978, pp. 33–6). Chancellor Lawson's 1984 budget led to the withdrawal of relief on *new* life assurance contracts but the relief continues on existing contracts. The example of tax relief on life assurance shows that we should not assume subvention is a recent development. In this connection it is worth observing that the complex of tax reliefs on occupational pensions was largely in place from 1921 (Willis and Hardwick, 1978, pp. 28–31).

At various stages in the argument so far we have compared the direct cost of public expenditure on income maintenance with the indirect cost of tax subvention on private saving. In his canonical 1955 essay on 'the social division of welfare', Titmuss (1976) insisted on such comparisons and analysed their salience. For Titmuss, occupational pensions were the main part of a tax-subvented system of private welfare which paralleled the transfer payment system of state welfare that had been re-designed on the lines recommended by Beveridge in *Social Insurance*. From this point of view, Titmuss questioned the hitherto conventional identification of 'welfare' with the direct state expenditure on income maintenance and social services. Indirect state subsidy of private income maintenance was undertaken for the same purposes and with the same results and should therefore be taken into account whenever welfare was discussed. The fundamental unity of direct and indirect expenditure was apparent not only in the case of old age pensions but also in the case of state aid for parents with dependent children. A public system of transfer payment 'family allowances' on the second and subsequent children was introduced in 1946. But an income tax allowance for dependent children was introduced as early as 1909 and extended to all taxpayers in 1920.

> Under separately administered social security systems, like family allowances and retirement pensions, direct cash payments are made in discharging collective responsibilities for particular dependencies. In the relevant accounts, these are treated as 'social service' expenditure since they represent flows of payments through the central government account. Allowances and reliefs from income tax, though providing similar benefits and expressing a similar social purpose in the recognition of dependent needs, are not however, treated as social service expenditure. The first is a cash transaction; the second an accounting convenience. Despite this difference in administrative method, the tax saving that accrues to the individual is, in effect, a transfer payment. In their primary objectives and their effects on individual purchasing power there are no differences in these two ways by which collective provision is made for dependencies. (Titmuss, 1976, pp. 44–5)

These arguments opened up much more than an academic debate about where the boundaries of the welfare system should be drawn. With the myth of 'private saving' disposed of and the reality of tax-subvented private welfare established, Titmuss was able to make a new kind of analysis of the conditions of existence and effects of private welfare.

On the question of conditions of existence, Titmuss argued that the private welfare system is occupational in that its major benefits (pensions, company cars, sick pay continuation, etc.) are restricted to those who hold certain occupational position. Although Beveridge and *Voluntary Action* was never mentioned by Titmuss, the implication of his argument is that Beveridge greatly overestimated the potential of voluntary association and underestimated the potential of workplace organisation as a basis for private welfare. Titmuss argued that the private welfare system is also fiscal because the value of its private benefits is enhanced by tax concessions which ensure that its benefits are not taxed or not taxed realistically. As for effects, the crucial point is that the system of occupational cum fiscal welfare is generally an 'accelerator of inequality' and it has regressive effects on the distribution of income. The major occupational benefits 'function as concealed multipliers of occupational success' because they go to privileged work groups and high-income individuals. Most of the fiscal concessions work in the same direction in an even more marked way because, under any progressive tax system, fiscal benefits will be worth more to the more affluent who pay higher rates of tax.

In the field of the 'social', the Titmuss essay marks a decisive break with the problematic of liberal collectivism. He was writing in the 1950s at a time when the 'welfare state' was being attacked on the grounds that the sphere of state social action was too large, too costly and promoting an excessive redistribution towards the less well off; Powell, Macleod and others were arguing that generous, universal welfare benefits were being provided for the working class at the expense of an overburdened middle class. Titmuss challenged this by showing that while the middle-class ideologues protested about the burden of direct state expenditure on public welfare, their middle-class social constituency was the main beneficiary of large indirect state subvention of private welfare. This argument was initially focused on social security versus occupational pensions. We have since discovered that, in other ways, the middle classes are doing quite nicely out of state expenditure. Le Grand (1983) brings together a variety of specialist work which shows the middle classes benefit disproportionately from public expenditure on housing, health and education.

At the same time our perception of inequality has changed so that the Le Grand-type inter-class comparisons of top to bottom inequality between middle- and working-class groups already seem a little dated. We are now increasingly concerned with intra-class and gender inequalities. The work of Atkinson (1984) and others shows that there is much scope for intra-class differentiation in pay, conditions and welfare fringe. The old patterns of white-collar versus blue-collar inequality are modified as employers increasingly try to buy the loyalty of key groups of primary workers within the working and middle classes. At the same time, we have become increasingly conscious of gender inequalities which disadvantage women. If Titmuss himself was sensitive to these issues, his generation tended to accept gender inequalities as natural and taken for granted. Thirty years have passed and much has changed since Titmuss wrote his 1955 essay. It is therefore worth updating and re-evaluating the evidence on how occupational pensions continue to act as accelerators of inequality.

Before we turn to the evidence, it is necessary to make some preliminary points about why it is difficult to generalise about the general effects of occupational pension schemes. To begin with, there are many different kinds of scheme. The situation has been considerably complicated by the way in which the state now provides its own earnings-related pensions. For thirty years after 1945 the state paid flat-rate state pensions as recommended by Beveridge. But in 1975 the state introduced a system of compulsory earnings-related old age pensions under the State Earnings Related Pensions Scheme which the Thatcher government now proposes to reform. Where there is no occupational scheme, employees earning above a very low earnings limit (£35.50 a week in 1983) are enrolled in the state scheme which is intended as a basic fall back. If there is an occupational scheme, employees can be either 'contracted in' or 'contracted out' from the state scheme. Where the employee is contracted in, the private scheme tops up the state earnings-related pension which is earned because both employee and employer pay the full national insurance contribution. Where the employee is contracted out, both employer and employee pay a reduced national insurance contribution, usually termed an 'abatement'. In return for this concession, the private scheme then undertakes to provide an earnings-related pension which is broadly no worse than the member would have obtained in the SERPS scheme and the state takes over certain responsibilities for inflation-proofing this pension. All this introduces major complications because private scheme members can stand in a variety of relations to the state scheme. However, matters are simplified because the vast majority of pension schemes are contracted out; in 1979 51 per cent of employees were members of private pension schemes and 44.5 per cent of employees were in contracted out schemes (Government Actuary's Department, 1981).

Even if most schemes are 'contracted out', it is still difficult to generalise because the sphere of private saving is a substantially unregulated one. Private pension schemes have a great deal of latitude when it comes to setting the rules and regulations which determine entitlement. The state directly sets only upper and lower limits on the entitlement of scheme members. At the upper limit, the Inland Revenue allows an occupational scheme to offer up to and no more than two-thirds of final salary as a pension. At the lower limit, a contracted out scheme must only provide a pension which is broadly no worse than the employee would have received from the state SERPS scheme. Both the upper and lower limits exist because the state aims, in a minimal way, to control the distributional effects of occupational pensions as accelerators of inequality. The upper limit curbs the extent to which occupational pension schemes can be used as a method of tax avoidance; the two-thirds ceiling simply limits the extent to which scheme members can avoid tax on income now by turning it into untaxed capital which can be drawn in the form of a

pension at some later date. The lower limit takes as its object hori-
zontal equity and a guaranteed minimum return; that is the point of
the stipulation that no scheme member should be disadvantaged
relative to SERPS. But, within the upper and lower limits, the state
sets no rules although scheme members do generally have considerable
advantage over non-scheme members and this has considerable distributional implications.

It might be thought that private occupational pension schemes do
at least treat the members who are within their schemes fairly because
although they make many of their own rules, these are universal rules
which apply to all scheme members. But this is not so because, as we
shall now argue, many of the universal rules contain an implicit
occupational model. These rules ensure greater benefits for the middle-
class individual who is well paid and increasingly well paid relative
to working-class counterparts over a working life because the middle-
class individual is likely to be on a rising salary scale within the firm
even if he is not promoted through the firm. It is true that occupational
pensions are to some extent a game of snakes and ladders for the
middle-class careerist; individuals who move between firms and pension schemes leave behind 'frozen' pension rights which will be worth
very little after twenty or thirty years of even moderate inflation. The
government's proposals for 'portable pensions' will help with this
problem which has been much emphasised in the press, partly no
doubt because journalists are one of the occupational groups most
affected. But the more important point is that for the averagely
immobile middle-class individual, the universal rules of his company
pension schemes ensure considerable advantage over the worse paid
manual worker in the same firm. The dice are loaded so that the
middle-class player usually lands on a square with a ladder.

By way of example, we will consider private scheme rules about
which year's earnings are taken into account when computing the
value of pensions. In an earlier period most private sector occupational
schemes based the value of the pension on money purchase (the benefit
being whatever the contribution would buy) or an average salary
throughout service. But such formulae failed to deal with inflation
and occupational pension schemes responded to this problem by
putting the value of the pension on a 'final salary' basis, that is, the
individual's pension is determined as a ratio to the earnings of that
individual at the end of his working life. In 1971 only 63 per cent of
occupational scheme members were in final salary schemes but by
1979, 91.8 per cent of private sector members had pensionable earnings calculated in this way (Government Actuary's Department, 1981,
Table 8.4). The Inland Revenue offers pension funds a variety of
options about how 'final salary' may be calculated; the scheme may
take any one of the five years' salary prior to retirement or an average

of three consecutive years in the ten preceding retirement. It is also worth noting that variations on a final salary rule are not the only way whereby a pension scheme can deal with a problem of inflation. The State SERPS scheme relates pension value to the revalued sum of average earnings over the 'best twenty years' of a working life. Furthermore, on our reading of the 1975 Social Security Pensions Act (sections 34(2), 34(5)) it is legally possible for private schemes to operate using a best twenty years rule. Instead almost all private schemes choose a final salary rule.

This is a case where we have an implicit occupational model. Maximum benefit from such a scheme will necessarily apply where the employee's pensionable earnings peak at the end of their working life. This feature has led some commentators to argue categorically that such schemes are particularly disadvantageous to *male manual* workers. For example, James argues:

> Over the years, pension funds have moved to base their pension on the final year's salary of the individual member. This is particularly beneficial for the career manager or professional worker. It is less suitable for other workers .... The wages of manual workers over 60 are about 15 per cent lower than for those between 30 and 50, when the individual is fitter and prompted by the demands of family and home to do more overtime, to produce more on bonus or piece rates. (James, 1984, pp. 11–12)

The importance of overtime and payment by results for manual workers does suggest that such workers will be disadvantaged by final salary rules. It is certainly the case that there is a sharp contrast between the role of such fluctuating payments in the earnings of manual and non-manual workers. For instance, the 1984 New Earnings Survey reveals that just over 25 per cent of the average weekly earnings of full-time male manual workers came from overtime payments, payments by results and shift premiums; the corresponding figure for non-manual full-time males was 7.6 per cent (Department of Employment, 1984). However, it is not correct to argue from this that the earnings of 'retirement age' non-manuals are closer to the earnings of younger non-manuals than is the case for manual workers. The highest earnings of full-time male non-manual workers occur in the 40–49 age group at £241.2; in contrast average earnings of the 60–64 group were £198 or 82 per cent of the peak (Department of Employment, 1984, p. E84). By comparison, earnings of full-time male manual workers peaked in the age range 40–49 at £164. The average for the 60–64 age group was 87 per cent of this at £143 (*ibid.*, p. E63). There are various reasons why figures drawn from the New Earnings Survey are in this respect inconclusive. Fundamentally, the form of the data is unsuitable for assessing the significance of final salary schemes to different groups of employees. This is because it is a cross-section, that is, it presents the earnings of *individuals* of *different ages* at a given point in time. In contrast, what is required would be data on *cohorts* of different occupational groups. From cross-section data on different groups of individuals we can draw no conclusion as to the earnings profile of occupational groups.

However, there is clearly an argument that final salary schemes are likely to disadvantage scheme members with weaker labour market position and/or a pattern of fluctuating earnings, since a variety of other more technical universal rules within pension schemes operate to reinforce the bias against worse-paid manual workers. By way of example we will consider the practice of 'integration' in contracted out schemes whereby a deduction from pensionable earnings is made to take account of the fact that every scheme member will also receive a basic pension from the state. This practice is fairly widespread; a Government Actuary's Department survey (1981) showed that in 1979 48.6 per cent of members of occupational schemes in the private sector were in schemes which practised integration. No information is available on the proportion of members in integrated schemes in the more up-to-date National Association of Pension Funds Survey of 1983. However, this survey showed that 54 per cent of schemes surveyed were integrated and, since the larger schemes were more likely to be integrated, this almost certainly understates the percentage of members in such schemes. Poorly paid workers suffer under the practice of integration which is regressive in its effects because the percentage reduction in pensionable earnings falls as income rises. To illustrate this point, in Table 2.2 we have taken various points in the

Table 2.2   Percentage cut in pensionable earnings produced by integration deductions in respect of state pensions

Rank in earnings league	Per cent cut in pensionable earnings	
	(a) *with lower earnings limit deduction*	(b) *with 1.5 times lower earnings limit deduction*
Men		
Upper quartile	16	24
Median	21	32
Lower quartile	27	41
Lowest decile	34	51
Women		
Upper quartile	24	36
Median	32	48
Lower quartile	40	60
Lowest decile	48	72

earnings hierarchy for men and women derived from the New Earnings Survey, 1984 and then assumed, first, a reduction from pensionable earnings of a sum equivalent to the 'lower earnings limit' for the year, and second, a reduction of one and a half times this figure which is the limit which may be deducted for these purposes under section 34(9) of the 1975 Social Security Pensions Act.

The regressive nature of integration is quite clear from this table; in the case of both sexes, the percentage cut in pensionable earnings for someone earning the upper quartile figure would be about half that for the lowest decile earner.

In a variety of ways, therefore, worse-paid manual workers are penalised by the operation of scheme rules if they are enrolled in the same pension scheme as their better-paid non-manual co-workers. Under a system of more explicit discrimination a significant minority of manual workers are enrolled in a separate 'works scheme' while their managers and supervisors are enrolled in staff schemes which offer better entitlements. This situation persists because in Britain no state regulations prevent employers from setting up two or more pension schemes which offer different benefits to groups of employees. In other impeccably capitalist countries, superior staff or top hat/senior management pension schemes are outlawed; the IRS in the USA, for example, insists that if employers give benefits in the form of pension rights, the same benefit should be given to a substantial majority of the workforce. In Britain the only pressure for 'combined schemes' comes from the widespread feeling that the staff/works distinction is outdated and divisive. But no doubt because pension entitlement involves money as much as (or more than) status, the distinction between staff and works pension schemes is remarkably persistent. The NAPF survey in 1983 showed that a clear majority (63 per cent) of all occupational pension scheme members were now enrolled in combined schemes. But that still left over a third of all occupational pension members in distinct staff or works schemes – 18 per cent in staff schemes and 19 per cent in works schemes (NAPF, 1984).

Staff schemes exist quite explicitly to offer superior entitlements to non-manual workers. If that is their *raison d'être*, the NAPF survey shows that staff schemes do achieve this aim. Table 2.3 shows that a poorly paid manual worker earning under £5,000 per annum who was enrolled in a works scheme could expect a pension which was just over 20 per cent of final salary after twenty years' contribution. An average (to poorly) paid manager or professional earning £11,000 to £15,500 who was enrolled in a staff scheme could expect a pension which amounted to nearly one-third of his much larger final salary after twenty years' service.

Differences in final pension entitlement are not the end of the matter

Table 2.3   Average pensions payable to members with twenty years' pensionable service in staff, works and combined schemes, 1983

Final eligible earnings £	Pension in £ and as per cent of final eligible earnings			
	Staff schemes	Works schemes	Combined schemes	All schemes
£4,500 per annum	£1,323.68	£943.74	£1,150.96	£1,193.10
	%29.42	%20.97	%25.58	%26.51
£11,000 per annum	£3,450.29	£2,577.27	£3,133.40	£3,191.13
	%31.37	%23.43	%28.49	%29.01
£15,000 per annum	£4,952.50	£3,671.47	£4,515.80	£4,586.40
	%31.95	%23.69	%29.13	%29.59
Overall average accrual rate per annum as % of final earnings	%1.54	%1.13	%1.38	%1.42

Source: NAPF Survey 1984

because staff employees do better in a variety of other ways. Consider, for example, the provision for death in service which is pertinent because a significant minority of scheme members die in middle age before they can claim any pension. Yet again, this is an area where state regulation is exiguous and permissive in Britain. In case of death in service, Inland Revenue rules allow schemes to pay a tax free lump sum to the surviving spouse; the lump sum can be varied between a lower limit of £5,000 and an upper limit of four times the dead employee's final salary. In practice, replies to the NAPF Survey (1984) show that, within this framework, staff schemes offer consistently superior death benefits. As is indicated in Table 2.4, more than half those enrolled in staff schemes in 1983 could expect that, if they died in service, their surviving spouse would receive a tax free lump sum equal to three or four years' salary. More than two-thirds of those enrolled in works schemes in the same year could expect a lump sum

Table 2.4   Lump sum payable following death in service by type of scheme

	Staff	Works	Combined	All
Lump sum equivalent to:	%	%	%	%
less than two years' salary	11	36	11	14
at least two years' but less than three years' salary	29	34	32	32
three years' but less than four years' salary	25	12	18	20
four years' salary	27	4	17	19
other	8	14	22	15

Source: NAPF survey, 1984

Table 2.5   Death rates (per 100,000 men): men 45–64

	45–64	55–64
Industrial managers	559	1,680
Professional workers (employees)	512	1,759
Foreman/supervisor non-manual	465	1,494
Junior non-manual	832	2,130
Personal service workers	1,069	2,608
Foreman/supervisor manual	514	1,747
Skilled manual	784	2,417
Semi-skilled workers	828	2,333
Unskilled workers	1,079	2,659

Source: OPCS, *Occupational Mortality, 1970–72,* 1974

equal to less than three years' salary. The staff schemes tend to pay death benefit up to the limit of what the Inland Revenue will allow and the works schemes pay substantially less.

This inequality is rendered more poignant if it is set in the context of the marked differences in occupational mortality shown in Table 2.5. From Tables 2.4 and 2.5, it is clear that benefits for death in service are highest for spouses in least (relative) need and vice versa.

The substantial differences in benefits between staff and works schemes arise partly, of course, because staff employees usually pay a higher percentage of income as employee contributions. According to the NAPF survey, in 1983 employee annual contributions as a percentage of eligible earnings were 4.56 per cent in the case of staff schemes and 3.50 per cent in the case of works schemes (NAPF, 1984, p. 13). When neither staff nor works scheme members are free to choose their rate of contribution, this would be rough justice even if staff members paid the full cost of their superior benefits by their own contributions. Staff members do not do this because staff schemes benefit from markedly higher employer contributions. The NAPF survey indicated that in 1983 the average employer's contributions as a percentage of eligible earnings in contributory schemes was 12.18 per cent in staff schemes and 7.12 per cent in works schemes (NAPF, 1984, p. 14). From the employer's point of view, the higher contribution to a staff scheme is an investment in traditional status distinctions which offers a financial pay-off to staff employees. From the works employee's point of view this is just another piece of discrimination which accelerates inequality in a blatant way.

In considering how occupational pension schemes accelerate inequality, we have so far considered how all worse-paid manual workers are discriminated against by the universal rules within occupational schemes, and how some worse-paid manual workers are discriminated against by being segregated into inferior works schemes.

The third and strongest form of discrimination is established by exclusion from occupational schemes. Exclusion matters because virtually every worker who is enrolled in an occupational scheme has an advantage over a worker who is enrolled in the state SERPS scheme which is intended as a basic fall back. As we have seen, the lower limit regulation is that workers in occupational schemes should do no worse than workers in the state SERPS scheme. Most workers in occupational pension schemes do substantially better because the state scheme is technically set up so that it does not offer generous earnings-related pensions. This is technically guaranteed by two features of the state scheme. There is under this scheme a maximum period of twenty years over which contributory entitlement is built up and an accrual rate of one-eightieth per annum, so that an individual can only build up a twenty-eightieths or one-quarter pension entitlement in relation to his/her revalued best twenty years' earnings. Most occupational pension schemes are substantially more generous. In an average middle-class scheme, there will be a maximum period of forty years over which contributory entitlement is built up and an accrual rate of one-sixtieth per annum, so that an individual can build up a forty-sixtieths or two-thirds pension entitlement in relation to final salary. In private occupational schemes accrual rates of one-eightieth are only found in the poorest works schemes which are at the bottom of the occupational pension heap. There are complications which affect this basic comparison: for example, under the state scheme widows can within certain limits inherit the pension rights of their dead husbands. But the generosity of the SERPS scheme in this respect has been much exaggerated by those who want to make a case for its abolition.

When only half the working population are enrolled in occupational pension schemes, exclusion must be considered the most important mechanism of discrimination. It reinforces the discriminations which operate within and between schemes because scheme members are disproportionately drawn from the better-paid groups in the working population. This is illustrated by Table 2.6 below which is drawn from the General Household Survey of 1976, the last year when questions were asked on this topic. As can be seen, nearly 90 per cent of intermediate non-manual and professional workers are enrolled in pension schemes but less than 60 per cent of manual workers are enrolled. The relatively low percentage of managers in small establishments enrolled in pension schemes is interesting because it indicates that some workers at all levels are excluded because their employers do not run occupational pension schemes. Such schemes were pioneered in the public sector and by larger private employers; they are still by no means universal in smaller private firms. This 'size of firm' effect does not however explain low working-class enrolment in pension schemes. At the working-class level there is an important

Table 2.6 Percentage of full-time employees different socio-economic
groups covered by employers' pension schemes

Managers in large establishments	88
Managers in small establishments	59
Professional workers – employees	87
Intermediate non-manual workers	88
Junior non-manual workers	65
Personal service workers	49
Foremen and supervisors	73
Skilled manual workers	59
Semi-skilled manual workers	59

Source: General Household Survey, 1976

subset of employees who are discriminated against very directly
because they are non-scheme members who work for an employer
who does run a scheme for other grades of employees.

The subset of employees which is excluded even though their
employer does operate a pension scheme is particularly hard done by.
Via the employer's contributions, part of the firm's revenue is being
deployed solely to benefit the group who happen to be scheme
members. However, insofar as one can link this revenue to the labour
of employees, all members of the employed workforce contribute to
its creation (Reddin and Pilch, 1985, p. 47). In these circumstances,
excluded individuals are exerting themselves partly so as to accelerate
somebody else's inequality; this is a kind of involuntary philanthropy
from the poor to the rich which is the exact opposite of what Beveridge
envisaged. If the injustice of exclusion in these circumstances is flag-
rant, it is suffered by a large number of working-class individuals.
The 1979 Government Actuary's Department survey shows some 7.15
million employees working in organisations where the employer had
a scheme but where they were not members. From this gross total we
should deduct two million who are excluded on grounds of insufficient
length of service and who, if they are young, newly recruited workers,
can hope to join the employer's scheme at a later date. But the
deduction of two million still leaves a net total of 5.15 million who
are unjustly excluded from occupational pension schemes even though
their employer runs one. The injustice of this exclusion has attracted
little attention partly because many of those excluded are women
manual workers whose chances and expectations of an occupational
pension are low.

All the exclusions which we have considered operate against low-
paid manual workers and they operate particularly against women
workers who, as we shall see in chapter 3, are concentrated disproportionately in menial service work. As a result, there is a marked
difference in the extent of scheme membership among men and

women; nearly two-thirds of female employees in 1979 were outside
private pension schemes (Government Actuary's Department, 1981).
Again, the pattern of gender exclusion is obvious if we analyse the
composition of the subset of those who are excluded from a pension
scheme by an employer who does run one. The 5.15 million net total
in this subset included 1.9 million men and no fewer than 3.25 million
women, so that 14 per cent of male employees and 34 per cent of
female employees are in this position. The contrast is so striking that
we must examine the mechanisms which explain how women are
excluded from pension schemes and how they often derive little benefit
from the schemes of which they do become members. In both cases
the obstacle is the character of women's work.

Those women who do join occupational pension schemes often
derive little benefit from membership. To obtain maximum benefits
from an occupational pension it is desirable to have a largely unbroken
pattern of work, preferably with a single employer. Women are handi-
capped by their employment history which typically includes a significant break in employment linked with child rearing in general and
child minding of the under-5s in particular. A recent extensive survey
of women's employment histories illustrates this point. Martin and
Roberts (1984, Table 2.3) present cross-section data which shows a
participation rate of 88 per cent amongst women aged 16 to 19
(excluding full-time students) falling to 54 per cent between the ages
of 25 and 29 and rising to a second 'peak' of 78 per cent between the
ages of 40 and 44. Equally, the striking effect of a pre-school child on
participation rates was revealed (Martin and Roberts, 1984, Table
2.6). Women with a youngest child of 4 or under had a participation
rate of only 31 per cent, as against 64 per cent where the youngest
child was between 5 and 10 and 76 per cent where the youngest child
was between 11 and 15 years. But a large-scale and early return to
work does not help the married woman's chance of an occupational
pension because the married woman typically returns to part-time
work where the chances of a pension are very slim. From our point
of view, this pattern is significant because only a very small percentage
of female part-time employees are pension scheme members. The
Government Actuary's Department (1981) survey, for example,
showed that in 1979 only 8 per cent of female part-time employees
were members of occupational pension schemes. The Martin and
Roberts (1984) survey confirmed this result; 53 per cent of full-time
female employees surveyed were scheme members as against only 9
per cent of part-time women. To all intents and purposes, part-time
work means minimal earnings-related pension provision. For this
reason, women's increased labour force attachment does not translate
into reduced disadvantage in the occupational pension sphere.

The whole existence and character of the domain of private pensions signals the fatal intellectual limitations and contradictions of liberal collectivism which dreams of a minimalist state provision which will leave intact the sphere of free private contracts. The existence and character of the pensions domain also signals the romantic essentialism of Beveridge's belief in the potential of voluntary action in the service of the higher motives of mutuality and altruism. Private pensions represent substantially unregulated compulsory contracts in a sphere which is hardly private in the classic sense because it is massively tax-subvented. All this is not only an embarrassment for liberal ideologues but a practical problem for us all because, as we have argued, at every point private pensions have regressive repercussions for the distribution of income as they accelerate inequality. We would of course admit that what we have described is a secondary problem about the redistribution of income from employment via a pensions superstructure. The regressive effects of our private pension system would be palliated insofar as economic development in the medium and long run created an ever-larger proportion of more-skilled and better-paid jobs. The problem now, as we shall argue in the next chapter, is that this kind of benign secular process of occupational upgrading seems to have failed in Britain over the past twenty years. In the pension system, we now have a powerful accelerator of inequality operating in an economy where the trends in the composition of employment are producing more ill-paid, part-time service jobs.

3 The level and composition of employment in Britain

Keynes and Beveridge each in their separate spheres concluded that the crucial liberal principles could only be safeguarded by insisting upon the relaxation of some specified liberal practices. In particular a degree of state intervention in a market economy was, they argued, both unavoidable and necessary to maintain intact the essential capitalist framework. Post-war policies were mostly guided by this liberal collectivist approach which had been overwhelmingly shaped by the writings of Beveridge and Keynes. The object of the present chapter is to analyse the implications of this in the field of employment. We shall examine the assumptions about the level and composition of employment which are embodied in the works of Beveridge and Keynes; indicate their proposed methods of implementation; and see how far these were borne out, or thwarted, by the main trends in employment in Britain since the war.

The basic assumption made about the level of employment is clear and direct. Liberal collectivism both sought full employment as a policy objective and assumed full employment as a condition of social policy. These aspects, as was indicated in chapter 1, are made quite explicit in the key texts of the *General Theory* and *Social Insurance and Allied Services*. It is less widely noticed that the liberal collectivist approach made various crucial assumptions not only about the *level* of employment but also about its *composition*. This oversight is only partly explained by the fact that some of these assumptions are not made fully explicit. It is immediately obvious that the assumption made about the level of employment is vital to the relation between the economic and the social: the social insurance scheme could only work if unemployment could be contained within reasonable limits and long-term unemployment more or less abolished. The assumptions made about the composition of employment were, however, equally important in linking the economic to the social: the social security scheme was built around the notions that the typical worker was a male who normally earned sufficient to support himself and a family of at least one child.

Liberal collectivist presuppositions about the composition of

employment can be divided into two broad categories: those concerned with the social character of the labour force, and those relating
to the wage levels at which work would be available. It is convenient
to examine each in turn.

The presuppositions relating to the social character of the workforce
are most clearly indicated by Beveridge whose view of the labour
market was one characterised by the dominance of men and single
women. This view had two underpinnings. The first reflected the belief
that the patterns of economic activity which had been experienced in
the inter-war period would persist:

> At the last census in 1931, more than seven out of eight of all
> housewives, that is to say, married women of working age, made
> marriage their sole occupation .... There has been an increase in
> the gainful employment of married women since 1931, but the
> proportion so employed was probably little above one in seven
> before the present war. (Beveridge, 1942, hereafter *SIAS*, p. 49)

Clearly, female participation rates had risen dramatically during
the war but this was (implicitly) considered 'abnormal', thus the
participation rates of the pre-war period seemed the natural point of
reference. In *Full Employment*, Appendix C (written by Kaldor)
assumed that, in the post-war period, there would be 500,000 more
women in the working population relative to 1938, an assumption
which involved a marked *drop* from the levels of female economic
activity in the Second World War. Kaldor argues:

> This last assumption is not unreasonable, in view of the fact that
> about 2 and a half million women were stated to have been drawn
> into industry and the Forces in the course of the present war; while
> after the last war, the number of women remaining in industry
> (up to the time of the slump of 1921, at any rate) was stated to
> have been about 30–40 per cent of those additionally employed
> in the course of that war. (Beveridge, 1944, pp. 369–70)

The 'high' rates of economic activity amongst married women were
thus treated as an 'exceptional' feature of wartime.

This forecast of what would happen after the Second World War
was reinforced by Beveridge's view of marriage. This view was built
into the plan for social security which treated 'man and wife as a
team'. The husband's role was to be that of economic provider, the
wife's that of the child rearer; the latter task was the wife's 'vital but
unpaid service'. This division of labour is strongly implied by the
differences built into Beveridge's approach to 'interruption of earnings' in the cases of married men and married women. Whereas in

the case of men, 'interruption of earnings' was an evil to be averted, in the case of the married woman, 'her earning is liable to interruption by childbirth. In the national interest it is important that *the interruption by childbirth should be as complete as possible*' (*SIAS*, p. 49, our emphasis). All this followed from the original assumptions: children had to be cared for, this was the wife's role. If she were overly concerned to return to work then the child would suffer: equally, it was not the wife's earnings which were crucial, but the husband's.

A similar view was expressed in *Full Employment in a Free Society*, where the male is seen as breadwinner for the family unit:

> The Plan for Social Security is designed to secure, by a comprehensive scheme of social insurance, that every individual, on condition of working while *he* can and contributing from *his* earnings shall have an income sufficient for the healthy subsistence of *him* and *his* family, an income to keep *him* above Want when for any reason *he* cannot work and earn. (Beveridge, 1944, para. 1, our emphasis)

Beveridge also assembles various extracts from the book *Men Without Work* in which aspects of the social evil of unemployment are illustrated with the unconsciously chauvinistic statements of the unemployed:

> 'The wife works while I look after the home .... I earned good wages ... for years and we had saved fifty pounds when I lost my job. We have none of that fifty pounds today. ... Any long spell of unemployment leaves you with little to be proud of and much to be ashamed of. Our child is still too young to realise that it is her mother who works. We carefully keep her from knowing it.' (*ibid.*, para. 360)

With his usual inexorable logic Beveridge related this view of the labour market to the design of social insurance. The status of women changed upon marriage because they ceased to be subject to the risks of single women and faced a new set of risks:

> On marriage a woman gains a legal right to maintenance by her husband as a first line of defence against risks which fall directly on the solitary woman; she undertakes at the same time to perform vital services and becomes exposed to new risks including the risk that her married life may be ended prematurely by widowhood or separation. (*SIAS*, p. 49)

Married women were no longer thought, by Beveridge, to be dependent on their own earnings for subsistence. Consequently, again, this justified different treatment for the marriage partners. In the case of the male, compulsory insurance contributions were the order of the day because his was the income on which the family depended and, thus, the income which the social security system had to replace. However, since the married woman was an economic dependant and, correlatively, marginal to the labour force, then,

> during marriage most women will not be gainfully occupied. The small minority of women who undertake paid employment or other gainful occupation after marriage ... require special treatment differing from that of single women. *Such paid work in many cases will be intermittent: it should be open to any married woman to undertake it as an exempt person* (*SIAS*, p. 50, our emphasis)

On marriage Beveridge proposed that the married woman would lose any entitlement (on the basis of prior contributions) to unemployment and disability benefit in her own right. She might 'requalify' for this benefit by paying contributions after marriage but then she would only qualify at a reduced rate. In contrast, and in line with her prescribed role in the 'team', on giving up work on the approaching birth of a child, she would qualify for thirteen weeks' maternity benefit at *above* the rate of unemployment and disability benefit paid to men and single women (*idem*). The precepts and rules of the Plan for Social Security were thus congruent with the dictum of the Prayer Book: 'He maketh the barren woman to keep house: and to be a joyful mother of children.' Certainly it is explicit in Beveridge that the problem of employment was predominantly a problem of male employment, to a lesser extent of the employment of single women, and not-at-all a matter of the employment of married women.

The crucial economic premise was that, at least in respect of male employment, there would not be a problem of *low* wages deriving from the *composition* of employment. This view is present but left implicit in Keynes who dealt with employment mostly at an aggregate and highly abstract level. Beveridge is both more direct and more descriptive. He asserts that 'very few men's wages are insufficient to cover at least two adults and one child' (*SIAS*, p. 155). It is true that there are passages in *Full Employment in a Free Society* where he seems about to establish a link between a given *sectoral* composition of employment and low wages:

> To some industries entry is made difficult by requirement of special skill, by trade unionism, or by marked localisation; they recruit labour only to meet their demand and they are not subject to easy invasion from other industries which happen to be depressed. On the other hand, to some industries and particularly to the widely

> scattered service industries entry is relatively easy. In times of
> depression they are subject to invasion from other industries.
> (Beveridge, 1944, para. 71)

In the event, however, such comments do not give rise to any discussion of a potential low-wage problem.

The reason for this is that Beveridge and Keynes were essentially
concerned with the level of employment, the composition of which
was not considered to be problematic. The prime object of *Full Employment in a Free Society*, for example, was to argue that unemployment
fundamentally derived from deficiency of demand and that it should
be a basic obligation of the state to ensure that aggregate demand
was sufficient for 'full employment'. In so doing the reasonable expectation was that a seller's market for labour would be created and thus
the 'wage problem' of the post-war world would not be low wages
but, rather, inflationary wage settlements.

How were these conditions to be created? If Beveridge provides the
clearest guide to the social character of employment, it is Keynes who
offers the means to implement a full employment policy. Keynes
himself left no single document comparable to *SIAS* which could
be taken to represent his more or less comprehensive and concrete
proposals for government action against unemployment in the post-
war world. If we are concerned with Keynes's own development, then
our interest must initially focus on *How to Pay for the War* which was
first published as articles in *The Times* on 14 and 15 November 1939.
These articles represent Keynes's attempt to adopt his *General Theory*
apparatus to think through an economic problem which was fundamentally different from that of the 1930s.

The fundamentals of the new problem to which Keynes addressed
himself in 1939 were simple enough. A war economy necessarily
generates a high level of economic activity; incomes therefore increase;
but there is less for consumers to buy because a great deal of the
output has to be diverted for war purposes. The economic problem
which presented itself after 1939 was one of demand-side excess rather
than the supply-side deficiency which had characterised the inter-war
period. How was the new problem to be tackled? The usual solutions
were to rely on taxation and voluntary savings to remove the excess
purchasing power but the inadequacies of these methods showed up
in strong inflationary pressure and, even more seriously, in reduced
incentive to produce. The additional solution proposed by Keynes
was characteristically ingenious and, more germane for our purposes,
arose directly out of the stress he placed on the level of aggregate
demand in the economy. He suggested a system of forced saving by
which a progressively increasing proportion of income would be held
back, but part of this – the proportion progressively decreasing as

income rose – would be reimbursed after the war. The essence there-fore was to curb the level of aggregate civilian demand during the war, but then to unblock the demand at some later date 'when the resources of the community were no longer fully engaged. Such releases would help us through the first post-war slump' (Keynes, 1978, p. 49).

A modified version of the scheme was introduced in the 1941 budget proposals which included post-war credits – certificates, which were to be redeemable after the war, and which were given for part of the additional tax levies. In the event, the failure of the anticipated post-war depression ever to arrive (partly because of counter-measures inspired by Keynes) made the repayment of these credits a financial embarrassment. For our purposes it is more important to note that the scheme embodied Keynes's essential lesson of manipulating the level of total expenditure (in this case by redistribution over time) to avoid both inflation and deflation. The scheme, moreover, embodied this principle in a characteristically Keynesian fashion at a high level of macro generality minimising the degree of detailed state intervention.

With Keynes distracted by the problems of designing an inter-national economic order for the post-war world, he provided no *vade mecum* for post-war domestic economic policy. The main official document presenting policy proposals which were based on (or descended from) the *General Theory* was the 1944 White Paper on *Employment Policy*.

The White Paper is now mostly remembered, if remembered at all, for its first sentence committing the wartime coalition government to full employment: 'The government accept as one of their primary aims and responsibilities the maintenance of a high and stable level of employment after the war.' This first sentence is significant partly because it accepts and restates the *General Theory*'s definition of the problem; the master issue was the *level* of employment. A whole series of issues about the *composition* of employment were never discussed at all; there was complete silence about such questions as the balance between male and female employment, full-time and part-time employment, manufacturing versus service employment, high-wage versus low-wage employment, high-skill versus low-skill employment. In the Keynesian problematic of 1944 all this was invisible. When the problem is conceived in this way, the question of the composition can only be addressed as a structural and regional problem concerning local imbalances in the demand and supply of labour. Reflecting the experience and policy initiatives of the late 1930s, the White Paper presumed that government would have to take responsibility for the location of manufacturing industry so as to ensure that this fitted the geographical distribution and skill profile of the (mainly) male working

population. The post-war composition problem would be one of fitting
fitting together supply and demand in a country where male manufacturing employment would continue to predominate.

It is not argued that this concentration on the level, and neglect of
the composition, of unemployment was unreasonable or perverse in
1944. Indeed, it could plausibly be presented as a proper priority
given the inter-war experience. In the 1930s three-quarters of all
women workers were single and 70 per cent were under 35 years old.
Whereas two out of every five women were in paid employment, only
one out of every ten married women was so occupied (Table 3.7, page
78). The assumption about full-time employment being mainly for
males was thus not an unreasonable first approximation. It is,
however, necessary to stress the implication that presenting the issue
in this way meant that the problems arising from the composition of
employment were ignored in this crucial trend-setting document –
and have continued to be neglected for most of the post-war period.

In the White Paper itself much of the solution for unemployment
was seen as dependent on the general prosperity of the basic industries
(coal, steel, shipbuilding, engineering) which could be secured by a
government committed to maintain 'domestic expenditure at a high
level' (White Paper, 1944, p. 11). But it was also recognised that there
would be difficulties about maintaining 'a balanced distribution of
industry and labour', and – more crucially – it was accepted that
government action would be needed to deal with these difficulties.
Three broad lines of attack were suggested. First, the government
would aim to influence the distribution of industry. Under this head
a number of detailed proposals to affect industrial location were given.
Enterprises were to inform government of proposals for new factories
and the government would have both negative ('power to prohibit')
and positive ('special inducements') means of influence. These would
include use of existing munitions factories; encouragement of new
factory building; provision of factories suitable for small firms; use of
government contracts; government assistance in 'facilities for obtaining short-term and long-term loans and, where necessary, share capital'; and government provision of the necessary infrastructure (*ibid.*,
p. 12). Second, the government would 'encourage a redistribution of
labour by providing resettlement allowances and houses, at a rent
which is within the means of the average wage earner' (*ibid.*, p. 15).
Finally, there would be extensive schemes for retraining provided by
industry (with some government finance) and by the state. Such
schemes would facilitate the necessary shift from declining to expanding industries. Trainees were to receive allowances which would be
'completely divorced from the payment of unemployment benefit'
and be made available as soon as it was clear that the worker was

'not likely to be able to resume his former employment within a reasonable time' (*ibid.*, pp. 14–15).

These proposals, in combating the regional and structural rigidities which inter-war experience had shown to be a major source of long-run unemployment, dovetail with a crucial aspect of the whole Beveridge scheme for attacking poverty on a state insurance basis. It was fundamental to Beveridge that poverty arose from 'temporary interruptions to income' and he accepted social security would have to support that long-term dependence which would necessarily stem from old age and sickness. Any additional long-term dependence arising from, say, prolonged unemployment would threaten his social insurance system. The 1944 White Paper on *Employment Policy* was obviously directed towards averting this threat. For this purpose all its suggestions for dealing with 'industrial imbalance' were relevant but the proposals for training workers were particularly pertinent. After all, Beveridge had himself suggested the need for coercive retraining for those heading for long-term unemployment.

The White Paper also placed considerable emphasis on the need to build an international economic system which would allow stable expanding international trade. This international framework was seen as a prerequisite for domestic prosperity because it would 'make it possible for all countries to pursue policies of full employment to their mutual advantage' (*ibid.*, p. 3). Unsurprisingly the White Paper was classically liberal collectivist in its position on international matters. The task was to construct a suitable framework of institutions and exchange rates, and it was assumed that within such a framework free trade would produce stable and equilibriating flows of goods. There was no conception of the possibility that some of the advanced countries might organise manufacturing production significantly better than their rivals with the result that flows of manufacturing goods could become unbalanced. A more open analysis would have pondered why and how most European countries blocked off the inflow of cheap American consumer durables in the inter-war period, or how the industrialising countries of the late nineteenth century found it necessary to block off the inflow of British goods.

The new international order, like the internal structural problem, was, however, ultimately a side issue. Given the preoccupation with the level of employment, the central issue was how to keep the economy at a high level of activity through suitable domestic policies. It was accepted that this objective would be threatened if there was not a reasonable stability of wages and prices. On this central point, however, the White Paper called only for 'the joint efforts of the Government, employers and organised labour', and warned against union restrictive practices and employer combines (*ibid.*, p. 19). There was also a reiteration of the need for sufficient mobility of labour to

accommodate the requirements of technical and commercial change.
The prime necessity, however, was seen to be that of maintaining the
level of total expenditure and on this point there was a clear and
unequivocal commitment: 'The Government are prepared to accept
in future the responsibility for taking action at the earliest possible
stage to arrest a threatened slump.' This 'new responsibility' was
necessary because 'experience has shown that ... under modern conditions [the] process of self-recovery, if effective at all, is likely to be
extremely prolonged and be accompanied by widespread distress'
(*ibid.*, p. 16). All this could have been taken from the *General Theory*.

The question was how the government was to deliver on its general
commitment to maintain 'domestic expenditure at a high level'. It
was recognised that the task would be difficult because the two most
volatile elements of total expenditure – private investment and the
foreign balance – were the least amenable to government control.
None the less, with an expanding international economy, the careful
planning of government investment and a willingness to check and
reverse the decline in consumer expenditure which 'normally follows
as a secondary reaction to a falling off in private investment', the
latter could be substantially influenced (*ibid.*, pp. 17–18). The White
Paper then set out a variety of methods by which total expenditure
could be maintained. The use of interest rates would help although
monetary policy alone 'will not be sufficient to defeat the inherent
instability of capital expenditure', especially as high rates were more
effective in curbing booms than were low rates in periods of depression.
Investment could be influenced more directly by government encouraging private industry to plan their investment and through control
of public investment, although there were constraints on this since
most public capital expenditure was undertaken by local authorities.
Finally, consumer expenditure could be varied particularly by adjusting social insurance payments so that they would vary inversely
with the level of unemployment (*ibid.*, pp. 20–4). It was explicitly
emphasised that all these schemes did not involve 'deliberate planning
for a deficit in the National Budget in years of sub-normal trade
activity' (*ibid.*, p. 24). Some of the proposals, like the lowering of
interest rates, would in fact assist a budget balance as would the
general attainment of a high, stable level of activity. At the very least
budgets would still have to balance over a period of years.

The broad assumptions of liberal collectivism have now been set
out along with the main proposals for their implementation. Our aim
in this chapter is now to examine each of these in the light of trends
in both the level and composition of employment in post-war Britain.
It is convenient to begin with the implementation.

The White Paper undoubtedly represented a major step forward
in terms of its overall strategic aim but the instruments it proposed

hardly seemed adequate to the counter-cyclical task. The variation of public investment programmes had been proposed in the inter-war period. As the official response to the 1929 Liberal proposal for road building made clear, it was difficult enough to accelerate central government expenditure on road building; local authority-controlled expenditure or the investment programmes of nationalised public utilities were even more difficult to regulate. On the consumption side, the proposals for counter-cyclical variation of insurance contribution was James Meade's toy. It was not clear that this device was adequate to dealing with a major recession. It was politically unacceptable to sections of the government apparatus and, if operated crudely, would have undermined the Beveridge design. Furthermore, it was quite clear from the optimism about avoiding budget deficits that the White Paper did not contemplate that any of the available instruments for varying investment or consumption expenditure would be used in a really heroic way. The fact of the matter is that the White Paper willed the end of full employment but ducked most of the issues about means.

Disillusion with liberal collectivism's economic programme never set in during the 1940s, or for twenty years after, because full employment was sustained without resort to them (see Table 3.1). In these

Table 3.1 Registered unemployed, annual averages, Great Britain, 1950–1980

	Number (000s)			*Percentage*		
	Total	*Male*	*Female*	*Total*	*Male*	*Female*
1950	314	220	94	1.5	1.6	1.4
1960	346	248	98	1.5	1.7	1.2
1970	582	495	87	2.5	3.5	1.0
1980	1591	1129	461	6.7	8.1	4.7

Sources: 1950 and 1960, *British Labour Statistics Historical Abstract* 1886–1968, Tables 165–7; 1970 and 1980, *Employment Gazette*

unanticipated circumstances the Keynesian baggage could be set aside as 'not wanted on voyage'. Under the 1944 proposals (if they had been implemented) insurance contributions would have varied up or down with each 2 per cent shift in unemployment, but, in the entire quarter century after the war, unemployment never rose much above 2 per cent. The proposals for encouraging and rescheduling public and private investment were equally irrelevant in a long boom when business confidence was sustained and investment was maintained at high levels by private initiative. Objectively all this was underpinned by a twenty-year boom in international trade. Britain benefited absolutely from this boom which had a multiplier influence on domestic economy activity, even though the British lost in terms of relative share of world trade.

The key point is that post-war circumstances were very different from what Keynes had envisaged in 1936 or 1940 or the White Paper had envisaged in 1944. And the *level* of employment was more or less autonomously safeguarded for twenty-five years in Britain, as in all the advanced countries whatever the practices or prejudices of the economic policy makers. In this foolproof (even Treasury-proof) situation, the British invented 'Keynesianism' – techniques of limited intervention which 'fine-tuned' the level of aggregate demand through variations in income tax, purchase tax and hire purchase regulations. These techniques of limited intervention soothed the liberal collectivist conscience by establishing an exemplary indirect and limited intervention which was (in political and administrative terms) altogether less problematic than the 'socialisation of investment' which Keynes had originally proposed. But any claims of policy makers to have created and sustained the high level of domestic activity must be considered implausible. The policy changes, as Dow has shown, were small (Dow, 1964). Econometric tests also suggest that these changes were not a great force for good or ill in the economy (Kennedy, 1973). The question of whether or, more exactly, under what circumstances state-initiated consumption or investment expenditure changes could curb large-scale unemployment has never been practically tested in Britain. Ironically, by the time the long boom did collapse after 1974 much of the Keynesian baggage had been thrown overboard and the techniques of demand management had been renounced. But the analysis of the suggested policy instruments must cast some doubt on how great a loss was thus sustained.

The examination of the employment presuppositions is necessarily more complex than that of implementation methods, especially as we want to shift the terms of the argument so that it considers not just the level but the composition of both employment and unemployment. To begin, we will outline the main trends in the composition of employment in Britain since the war and we will discriminate the longer trends over the period 1950 to 1980 before separately considering the accentuation of these trends in the period of slump under the Thatcher administration since 1979.

To start with the basics and the longer view: the labour force grew persistently over the period 1950–80. The total working population rose from 23.0 million in 1950 to 26.2 million in 1980 (Table 3.2). A very broad distribution of this working population can be made by distinguishing the numbers in the primary, secondary and tertiary sectors, which we can roughly identify as agriculture and mining, manufacturing, and services. Table 3.3 presents two measures of the changes between these sectors. (They differ because of the different

Table 3.2   Total working population, 1950 and 1980, by sex, Great Britain

Year (June)	1950	1980
Employees in employment		
Male	13,447	13,018
Female	6,871	9,440
Total	20,318	22,458
Employees and self-employed		
Male	1,376	n.a.[1]
Female	318	n.a.[1]
Total	1,694	1,950
Wholly unemployed		
Male	196	1,024
Female	77	420
Total	273	1,444
HM Forces		
Male	673	n.a.
Female	24	n.a.
Total	697	323
Total working population		
Male	15,692	n.a.
Female	7,290	n.a.
Total	22,982	16,176

[1] n.a. = not available. Figures for 1979 are: self-employed males, 1,499; females, 343; total, 1,842 (*Employment Gazette*, July 1984).

Sources: 1950 *British Labour Statistics Historical Abstracts* (1971), Tables 121–3
1980 *Employment Gazette*, August 1984, Historical Supplement, p. 6

methods of collection and different definitions used by the Department of Employment and the Census.) They each show the same essential picture: a dramatic drop in the numbers engaged in the primary sector (agriculture and mining), a substantial decline in the numbers employed in manufacturing, and a large increase in the number in the service industries. The decrease in both the absolute numbers and in the proportionate share of the workforce engaged in primary production, although marked, was by no means particularly significant. By 1950 the number engaged in this sector was already relatively small and the decline represented the continuation of a trend which already went back well into the nineteenth century in the case of agriculture and to the 1920s in the case of mining. The trends in manufacturing employment are much more pertinent when the numbers involved are larger and the comparison between 1950 (8.3 m.) and 1980 (6.7 m.) disguises the sharpness of the fall. The

Table 3.3   Distribution of labour force by sector, 1950 and 1980

| | Employees in employment Numbers (000s) | | | | | |
	1950			1980		
	Male	*Female*	*Total*	*Male*	*Female*	*Total*
Agriculture and mining	1,509	128	1,637	595	198	648
Manufacturing	5,547	2,271	8,318	4,744	1,935	6,713
Services	6,391	3,972	10,363	7,492	7,135	14,940
Total	13,447	6,871	20,318	12,831	9,178	22,351
	As percentage of total					
	Male	*Female*	*Total*	*Male*	*Female*	*Total*
Agriculture and mining	11.2	1.9	8.1	4.6	1.2	3.1
Manufacturing	41.3	40.3	40.9	37.0	21.1	30.0
Services	47.5	57.8	51.0	58.4	77.7	66.8
	Census Numbers (000s)					
	1951			1981		
	Male	*Female*	*Total*	*Male*	*Female*	*Total*
Agriculture and mining	1,838	129	1,967	590	107	697
Manufacturing	5,369	2,528	7,897	4,216	1,656	5,872
Services	8,090	4,163	12,253	7,139	6,900	14,039
Total	15,309	6,826	22,135	11,945	8,663	20,608
	As percentage of total					
	Male	*Female*	*Total*	*Male*	*Female*	*Total*
Agriculture and mining	12.0	1.9	8.9	4.9	1.2	3.4
Manufacturing	35.1	37.0	35.7	35.3	19.1	28.5
Services	52.8	61.0	55.4	59.8	79.6	68.1

For 1950 and 1980, Primary (Agriculture and mining) = Industry orders I and II; Manufacturing = Orders III–XVI; and Services the remainder (1950 on 1948 SIC: 1980 on 1968 SIC)

Sources: 1950 *British Labour Statistics Historical Abstract*, 1971, Tables 135–7
1980 *Employment Gazette*, March 1981
Census figures calculated from Census returns for 1951 and 1981

numbers were rising through the first half of the 1950s, reaching a peak of 9.1 m. in 1956, and then declined gently for a further decade. In 1966 they were still at much the same level (8.4 m.) as they had been in 1950. Thus over one and a half million jobs were lost in manufacturing between then and 1980.

Does this simply reflect a general international trend? It is true that the decline in the relative importance of manufacturing is a general phenomenon of economic development, but the British decline from 41 per cent in 1950 (42 per cent in 1956) to 30 per cent in 1980 was more than usually precipitous. What really distinguishes the British case is the *scale* of the fall in absolute numbers. Table 3.4 shows how the proportion of the total workforce engaged in manufacturing is declining in all the main advanced industrial countries. In the US and Britain this proportional decline has been a persistent post-war feature; in Japan and Germany it dates from around 1970; and in France from the mid-1970s. But in terms of absolute numbers working in manufacturing, the British case is quite distinctive with its persistent and marked fall going back to the late 1950s. In the US the number was increasing until 1980 (and may yet go above that level again); in Japan, despite a little spluttering in the 1970s, the trend of the numbers continued to increase throughout; in France and West Germany the peak year was 1974. In France there was then a persistent fall of 900,000 over the next decade. In Germany there is after 1974 something which seems nearer to the British case – a fall from 10.7 m. in 1974 to 8.6 m. in 1983. But the pattern is very peculiar: the figures suggest that most of this (1.4 m.) took place in the single year from 1974 to 1975 suggesting an extraordinarily sharp and rapid response to the first oil crisis. Perhaps this was possible through the repatriation of immigrant 'guest' workers, which would also explain a decline of about one million in the total economically active population in Germany over the three years after 1974.

Finally, the British decline in manufacturing employment stands out because it is sustained on a broad front right across the manufacturing sector. Shifts in a large aggregated figure like that of 'manufactures' are usually the result of balancing winners against losers; the gains in some sectors are set off against losses elsewhere. But in Britain there are no winners. The fourteen broad industry groups contained within the manufacturing sector in 1950 can be matched against those for 1980 (there are some difficulties because the seventeen groups used in the 1980 figures have to be slightly rearranged but for this purpose the comparisons are clear enough). The fact is that only four of the industry groups recorded a gain. All the others registered a loss. The four exceptions – metal goods not elsewhere specified (n.e.s.), precision instruments, other manufacturing, and paper, printing and publishing – showed only very marginal gains accounting in total for just 100,000 jobs. The losses on textiles alone were more than six times as great whilst other areas like clothing and vehicles also registered very large losses (Table 3.5).

Opportunities for manufacturing employment in Britain, especially from the mid-1960s onward, were diminishing in a way and to an

Table 3.4 Number and percentage of workforce engaged in manufacturing, various countries, 1950–1983

	1950 No.	%	1960 No.	%	1970 No.	%	1975 No.	%	1980 No.	%	1983 No.	%
US	16,113	26.8	18,536	26.5	21,936	25.5	21,602	22.7	23,556	21.4	22,414	19.8
Japan	5,650	15.6	9,495	21.6	13,576	25.6	13,158	24.2	13,670	24.2	14,060	23.9
France	4,518	22.0[1]	5,178	26.4[3]	5,551	26.1	5,819	26.8	5,441	23.7	5,066	22.0
W. Germany	6,806	30.8	9,277	36.2	10,050	37.9	9,347	34.8	9,106	34.1	8,563	31.4
UK	8,446	37.4[2]	8,614	34.8[4]	8,136	32.6[5]	7,411	28.5[6]	6,929	26.3	n.a.	n.a.

[1] 1946 [4] 1966
[2] 1951 [5] 1971
[3] 1957 [6] 1976

n.a. = not available
Source: ILO *Year Book of Labour Statistics*, 1950–84. Table 2A (figures include employees, self-employed, and unpaid family workers)

Table 3.5 Total number of employees in employment by industry order, 1950 and 1980 (000s)

	1950	1980
Non-metalliferous mining other than coal	327	280
Chemicals and allied trades	469	436
Metal manufacture	541	399
Engineering, shipbuilding and electrical	1,786	1,767
Vehicles	981	699
Metal goods n.e.s.	493	518
Precision instruments, jewellery	137	147
Textiles	1,008	382
Leather, leather goods and fur	77	33
Clothing	658	319
Food, drink and tobacco	784	669
Manufacture of wood and cork	298	237
Paper and printing	510	539
Other manufacturing industries	250	288

Sources: 1950 *British Labour Statistics Historical Abstract*, 1971, Table 135
1980 *Employment Gazette*, March and October 1981

extent which was unparalleled in other manufacturing countries. This secular squeeze particularly affected working-class individuals who sought manual jobs because there was an appreciable shift in the balance of occupations within manufacturing. This can be seen in Table 3.6 which shows the split in manufacturing employment between 'operatives' on the one hand and 'administrative, technical and clerical staff' on the other. In 1950 83.5 per cent were manual workers but by 1980 this had fallen to 70 per cent. Figures on absolute

Table 3.6 Percentage of administrative, technical and clerical workers in manufacturing industries, Great Britain

1959	1966	1970	1974	1978	1980	1982
21.1	24.3	26.7	27.0	28.4	30.0	30.6

Source: Annual Abstract of Statistics, various issues

numbers are not available until the 1960s but then show a fall in the number of manual workers from 6.8 m. in 1962 to 4.5 m. in 1980. The administrative, technical and clerical staff experienced only a very mild decline from 2.0 m. to 1.9 m. over the same period; indeed, 1980 was the first year in which the non-manual staff fell below its 1962 level. Not only did employment decline in manufacturing but job loss was concentrated amongst manual workers.

In addition to, and partly as a consequence of, changes in the relative importance of the broad sectors of the economy, there was a major shift in the balance between the sexes in the labour force. The composition changes which we have analysed so far were working in favour of women and against men. As we have already noted, in the thirty years following 1950 the total working population rose by 3.2 m. (Table 3.2). The remarkable fact is that virtually the whole of this expansion came, statistically speaking, from the increasing numbers of women entering the labour force. Indeed, for the major component of these figures – employees in employment – the number of males actually fell slightly between these dates (from 13.4 m. to 13.0 m.), whilst the number of females rose from 6.9 m. to 9.4 m. This reflected, so far as women workers were concerned, two major trends: there was an increase in the female participation ratio (that is, a rise in the proportion of women aged between 15 and 60 who were economically active), and, more specifically, there was an increase in the number of older women at work (Table 3.7). Thus, while male manual workers faced an increasingly difficult jobs market, increasing numbers of married working-class women went out to work. The trend to rising female participation had not been, indeed could not have been, anticipated in the 1930s and 1940s. Rising female participation is a post-war phenomenon; as Table 3.7 shows, inter-war female participation rates look very like those of the early twentieth century.

Table 3.7   Percentage of women in the labour force: changes over time, England and Wales

	Percentage of working women aged:			Participation rate: % of group economically active		% of working women who were:		
	Under 35	35–59	60 and over	All women 15–59	Married women 15–59	Single	Married	Divorced or widowed
1901	73	22	5	38	10	78	13	9
1931	69	26	5	38	11	77	16	7
1951	52	43	5	43	26	52	40	8~
1971	40	52	8	55	49	28	64	8
1981	45	50	5	61	57	36[1]	64	

[1] Includes divorced and widowed
Source: Census Reports for England and Wales. Figures for 1901–71 taken from Catherine Hakin, *Occupational Segregation*, Dept. of Employment Research Paper no. 9, 1979

We may ask how working women were able to find jobs in a labour market which was increasingly difficult for men. The answer is that the men were caught in the declining manufacturing sector while the women found new opportunities in service employment. The additional women workers were in no way replacing men in manufacturing industry. Not only did the number of women in manufacturing fall alongside that of men between 1950 and 1980, but the proportional decline was actually twice as fast for women (30 per cent instead of 15 per cent in terms of employees in employment) (Table 3.3). The extra labour was entirely absorbed into the service industries but not evenly. There is a contrast between the so-called productive services (building and construction, gas, water and electricity, and transport and communications) and other service sectors. In each of the former total employment declined between 1950 and 1980. It was in the other service industries that employment increased (Table 3.8).

Table 3.8 Number of employees in employment, service industries, by sex, 1950 and 1980

Industry group	Date	Total	Male	Female
Building	1950	1,294	1,257	37
	1980[1]	1,237	1,122	197
Gas, electricity and water	1950	354	321	33
	1980	342	269	68
Transport and communications	1950	1,738	1,509	229
	1980	1,483	1,193	285
Distributive trades	1950	2,082	1,089	993
	1980	2,821	1,221	1,512
Insurance, banking and finance	1950	430	271	159
	1980	1,292	574	663
Public administration and defence	1950	1,369	984	386
	1980	1,539	936	608
Professional services	1950	1,422	499	922
	1980	3,658	1,140	2,469
Miscellaneous services	1950	1,657	444	1,212
	1980	2,571	1,038	1,423

[1] In each case the 1980 figures for male and female may not tally exactly with the total figure because the total figure was adjusted to take account of the 1981 Census of Employment. The differences do not affect the general points being made.
Sources: British Labour Statistics Historical Abstract, 1971, Table 135, and

The sectors of decrease were, however, all attributable to declines in male employment. Female employment rose in all these sectors – fairly modestly in the three productive services but quite dramatically in all the others, especially professional services where an additional one and a half million women were employed in 1980 compared to 1950 (mostly as teachers and nurses). Up until the end of the 1970s, therefore, a significant part of the increase in female employment took place in the public and professional sectors. As we shall see this ceased to be the case from 1980 onwards, and this represented a shift which was important for both the status and remuneration of working women.

With the rise in service employment for women, there were important changes in the age structure of occupied women. Table 3.7 has already indicated that, whereas at the beginning of the century almost three-quarters of the women at work were under 35, by 1981 over half were over 35. In 1901 some 61 per cent of women in the age group 15–24 were at work, but the participation rate then dropped, quite sharply at first to 31 per cent for those aged 25–34 and then more steadily. The current pattern is quite different. In 1981 (England and Wales) the youngest age group (16–24) still had a high participation ratio of 63 per cent which fell to 54 per cent for ages 25–34. But thereafter – in sharp contrast to the past – participation rose again to 65 per cent (35–44) and 66 per cent (45–54) before falling to 52 per cent for those aged 55–9. This is largely explained by the so-called 'bi-modal pattern', whereby most women work before marriage, leave the paid labour force whilst the children are young, but then return again to paid employment as children grow up (Hakin, 1979, p. 4). It is confirmed by the figures (Table 3.7) showing the upward trend in the participation rate for married women, and it is reinforced by the fact that there is now a higher participation ratio for married women in the 45–54 age bracket than in the 16–24 age group. Later studies have detected a more complicated pattern with women increasingly breaking away from the simple bi-modal behaviour and returning to work sooner after childbirth and between having children (Dex, 1984, p. 1). This further reinforces our general points about the post-war changes in the level and distribution of women's employment.

The return to the labour force for married women is eased by the ready availability of part-time work for women. Part-time work is usually defined as less than thirty hours a week. On this basis in 1950, 12 per cent of all women workers were part-time: by 1980 40 per cent were in this category (Table 3.9). The full significance of this only emerges if attention is drawn to the fact that it represents an increase between 1950 and 1980 of nearly three million part-time women workers and when we remind ourselves that the total British labour force grew in this period by about three million. So, broadly speaking, not only was all the post-war growth of the labour force made up of women, it was made up of women in part-time work.

The long-run trends in the composition of employment over the post-war period up to 1980 can now be summarised. They include the fact of a substantial decline in the importance of employment in

Table 3.9   Importance of part-time employment, males and females, Great Britain, 1951, 1971 and 1981

| | | Males | | | Females | |
		Total employed (000s)	Of which, part-time (000s)	Part-time as % of total	Total employed (000s)	Of which, part-time (000s)	Part-time as % of total
1951	All sectors	13,782	44	0.3	6,158	744	12.1
	Manufacturing	5,899	8	0.1	2,374	248	10.4
	Services	7,007	30	0.4	3,679	486	13.2
1971	All sectors	13,424	584	4.4	8,224	1,757	33.5
	Manufacturing	5,556	73	1.3	2,355	480	20.4
	Services	5,752	472	8.2	5,609	2,198	39.2
1981	All sectors	12,229	718	5.9	9,085	3,781	41.6
	Manufacturing	4,311	69	1.6	1,747	395	22.6
	Services	6,061	601	9.9	7,040	3,288	46.7

Sources: 1951 Census of Population; 1971 and 1981 Dept. of Employment, Census of Employment. Figures for different years are not exactly comparable. In particular 1951 uses both a different source and a different SIC. The 1971 and 1981 figures are based on employees in employment, the 1951 census figures on all employees. But none of this affects the broad trends with which we are mainly concerned. For each year the Table does not distinguish those in primary production, although they are included in the totals.

Table 3.10   Total working population, Great Britain, June quarter 1980, 1984

	Employees in employment 1980	1984	Employers and self-employed 1980	1984	Wholly unemployed 1980	1984	HM Forces 1980	1984	Total working population 1980	1984
Males	13,018	11,756			1,024	2,034				
Females	9,440	9,157			420	877				
Total	22,458	20,913	1,950	2,270	1,444	2,911	323	326	26,176	26,420

Source: Employment Gazette, December 1984.

manufacturing industry. There are some indications that the British experience was exceptional amongst advanced industrial countries because of its scale and because it represented a decline not only in the relative importance of manufacturing employment but also a much earlier and more decisive absolute decline in the numbers working in manufacturing industry. Moreover, within this sector the proportion of male manual workers was declining. In terms of the total working population the outstanding fact is that for this entire generation the only source of increase in the labour force was the extra number of women in paid employment, a trend that was mostly accounted for by the strong growth in the number of older and married women at work. Virtually all the increase, however, was made up of women in part-time employment mostly in the poorly paid lower grades. Statistically, too, all these women (and more) were engaged in the service industries.

For much of the post-war period the effects of the adverse trends in the composition of employment were masked by the maintenance of a high level of employment. Indeed, the post-war experience of unemployment was unusually favourable. Not until the second half of 1976 did the number of unemployed creep above one million, and as late as 1980 the annual average for male unemployment in Great Britain still only just reached 8 per cent: in designing his insurance scheme, Beveridge had assumed that unemployment would *average* 8.5 per cent amongst manual workers (*SIAS*, pp. 164, 185). At the same time the change in the pace and scale of unemployment growth in the 1970s was unmistakable. The number out of work trebled during the decade, despite the fact that the total working population actually fell during these years.

The effects of the changes in the composition of employment thus became more difficult to ignore, especially as the pace of these changes accelerated in the 1980s. All this is very clear if we examine the composition of employment (and unemployment) in the most recent period since 1980. For the first few years the total working population was basically static. This reflected not demographic trends but a fall in the male participation rate caused by the 'discouraged worker' effect which led elderly males in particular to withdraw completely from the labour market. From about 1983 the working population then grew mostly because of a renewed rise in female participation rates. In all, the total working population rose by about 250,000 between 1980 and 1984. The increase, however, disguised quite substantial changes in the constituent parts (Table 3.10). There was a large proportional rise of over 300,000 (1.95 m. to 2.27 m.) in the number of employers and self-employed, but the number of employees in employment fell by just over 1.5 m. and the total number of unemployed rose by just under 1.5 m.

The composition of both the unemployed and the employed populations is instructive. Let us begin with the numbers out of work. Unemployment has everywhere risen massively despite deliberate government massaging to reduce the figures, and also disregarding the half-million or so who, by mid-1985, were on government make-work schemes. But from our point of view it is equally significant that that the rises have in a number of respects been unevenly distributed, and this unevenness naturally reflects changes in the composition of unemployment.

It is true that differences in regional unemployment rates have followed a generally consistent pattern. Throughout the post-war period, the North of England, Northern Ireland, Wales and Scotland exhibit much higher rates than the South East. But the levels in all the regions substantially increased in the 1980s. Unemployment rates in some regions have quite literally reached 1930s levels. For example, in November 1985 unemployment in Northern Ireland was 21.3 per cent and in the North of England 17.9 per cent (seasonally adjusted). The one exception to a consistent long-run pattern is the sharp increase in the traditionally low unemployment of the West Midlands region. In November 1985 unemployment in this region was above the national average at 14.9 per cent (see also Table 3.11). This serves as a clear indication of the decline in manufacturing: low unemployment and prosperity had for long been sustained in this region by a diversified manufacturing base.

The social composition of the unemployed also shows predictable variation. This emerges from a brief examination of the differences in terms of sex and age. In mid-1985 the male unemployment rate was heading towards double that of women (15.8 per cent against 9.3). The figure for women was understated because the regulations often made it not worth their while to register but the lower percentage clearly does also reflect the readier availability of women's work. Unemployment is also heavily concentrated amongst the younger age groups who cannot 'get started' in a difficult jobs market. Table 3.12 shows that unemployment in the 18–24 age group is one and a half to twice the average of other age groups. At the other end of a working life, older employees are another vulnerable age group because their prospects of re-employment are slim. The older employee approaching retirement age often does not become unemployed but leaves the labour force. This trend is particularly marked amongst men and has been enormously accelerated during the Thatcher years: the economic activity rate among men aged 60 to 64 was 85 per cent in 1973, 75 per cent in 1978, and had collapsed to 57 per cent in 1984 (*Social Trends*, 16, 1986, and *General Household Surveys*, 1976).

The social characteristics of the unemployed thus have to be added to the overall unemployment situation which dramatically worsened

Table 3.11 Proportion of unemployed, by age and duration, Great Britain, and unemployment rate by regions, April 1985

(a)

Proportion of unemployed out of work for:			Proportion of unemployed in each age group:		
	Male	*Female*		*Male*	*Female*
under 2 weeks	4.7	6.0	under 18	4.1	6.9
2–8 weeks	9.9	12.3	18-24	29.0	39.0
8–26 weeks	21.3	26.1	25–34	23.5	23.9
26–52 weeks	19.5	24.7	35–44	16.3	11.4
1–2 years	17.2	15.3	45–54	13.8	11.7
2 years +	27.4	15.5	55–59	9.8	6.9
			60 +	3.5	0.1

(b)

Unemployment rate by regions

Region	Male	Female	Total
South-east	11.8	7.4	9.9
Greater London	12.5	7.6	10.5
East Anglia	12.2	8.8	10.8
South West	13.8	9.7	12.0
West Midlands	18.1	11.5	15.5
East Midlands	15.1	9.5	12.8
Yorkshire and Humberside	17.7	10.9	15.0
North West	20.0	11.2	16.2
North	23.1	12.7	18.8
Wales	20.6	11.7	16.9
Scotland	19.2	11.1	15.7
Northern Ireland	26.8	13.4	21.0

(c)

Number and per cent unemployed, 1980 and 1984

	1980	1984
Male no.	1,129	2,110
%	8.1	15.5
Female no.	461	929
%	4.7	9.3
Total no.	1,591	3,039
%	6.7	12.9

Source: Employment Gazette, June 1985

Table 3.12 Percentage unemployment rates by age (October 1984)

U/18	18–19	20–24	25–34	35–44	45–54	55–9	60 +
27	26.5	19.5	12.8	8.4	8.4	11.4	14.6

Source: Employment Gazette, Sept. 1985

after 1979. In the mere four years between 1980 and 1984 the total number unemployed in Great Britain increased by nearly one and a half million. The rise was, moreover, associated with the emergence of a major problem about long-term unemployment – by 1984 over 40 per cent of the men and 30 per cent of the women who were unemployed had been without a job for over a year.

Similarly the broad trends in the composition of employment mostly continued and quickened from 1980. In broad sectoral terms the

Table 3.13   Distribution by sector, employees in employment, Great Britain 1980 and 1984 (June)

| 1980 | Numbers (000s) | | | Per cent | | |
	Male	Female	Total	Male	Female	Total
Agriculture and mining	586	105	690	4.6	1.1	3.2
Manufacturing	4,731	1,929	6,660	37.0	21.1	30.4
Services	7,448	7,106	14,555	58.3	77.7	66.5
Total	12,765	9,140	21,905			
1984						
Agriculture and mining	492	97	588	4.1	1.1	2.8
Manufacturing	4,173	1,572	5,744	34.9	17.2	27.2
Services	7,294	7,497	14,793	60.9	81.6	70.0
Total	11,959	9,166	21,125			

Source: Employment Gazette, October 1980 and December 1984

relative decline of agriculture and mining, and of manufactures, continued and the relative importance of employment in the service industries increased (Table 3.13). By 1984 three out of every five employed men were in the service sector (including the so-called 'productive' services of transport, construction, and public utilities), and four out of every five women were so employed.

A few other facts stand out. Several of them reflect the influence of a general recession which affected the national manufacturing sector particularly severely. Manufacturing output fell by nearly 10 per cent in the single year 1979–80 and by a further 6 per cent from 1980 to 1982, and the vaunted recovery had still by 1984 failed to restore manufacturing output even to its 1980 level (*Employment Gazette,* December 1984, Table 1.8). Taking the Thatcher years as whole, the overriding fact is that the pace of manufacturing decline sharply quickened. It has already been remarked that Britain was unusual before 1980 in exhibiting not just a decline in the relative importance of manufactures but a marked fall in the absolute numbers employed in this sector. This arose from the loss of 1.5 m. manufacturing jobs in the dozen years before 1980: but the mere four years after 1980 saw a further decline of one million. Interestingly, the decline in manufacturing employment was, proportionately, greater for women workers (19 per cent against 12 per cent for men). The trend for women, however, partly reflects a growing tendency by manufacturing firms to contract out tasks like cleaning and catering. In some of these cases it was possible for the same women to be doing the same job in the same place but, as they were now employed by an outside contractor, they would now be classified under services instead of manufacturing.

It should be added as a cautionary comment that it is quite normal for manufacturing employment (and output) to be more affected by economic slump than is the case in service industries. In the US, for example, there was an absolute decline in the numbers working in manufacturing during the general recession of 1980–1 – but the numbers rose again from 1982 onwards. In Britain the absolute decline though decelerating seems to have continued throughout. As already indicated a million jobs were lost in manufacturing in the four years of both recession and recovery from 1980 to 1984. The comparison would be even worse with 1979; between December 1979 and March 1983 nearly one and a half million manufacturing jobs were lost. Recovery, at best, has reduced the rate of outflow: between March 1983 and the spring (April) of 1985 a further 200,000 jobs were lost in manufacturing. During the Thatcher years the relative decline in the significance of manufacturing has been of the order of an alarming 1 per cent per annum.

The general decline in activity in Britain in the 1980s did affect the service industries where the total number employed stagnated up to 1984. Before 1980 only the 'productive' services (construction, transport, and utilities) had declined and they continued to do so from 1980–84 but in the latter period they were joined by professional and miscellaneous services. Public administration was a stagnant area. There were only two sectors of substantial growth: distributive trades; and insurance, banking and finance (Table 3.14). Before 1980 all eight sectors had seen increasing female employment but this was now reversed for half of them (public utilities, transport, professional services, and miscellaneous services). The only large expanding sectors for female employment after 1980 were the distributive trades, and

Table 3.14 Employees in employment, service sector, June 1984

Industry group	Total	Male	Female	Female part-time
Building	975	856	119	54
Gas, electricity and water	318	255	62	2
Transport and communications	1,298	1,036	262	55
Distributive trades	4,289	1,957	2,323	1,410
Insurance, banking and finance	1,875	969	906	262
Public administration and defence	1,544	839	705	219
Professional services	2,969	870	2,098	1,114
Miscellaneous services	1,525	505	1,021	631

Source: Employment Gazette, December 1984, Table 1.4

insurance, banking and finance. In each of these, and in the service industries as a whole, there was, moreover, a reinforcement of the trend towards part-time work. By 1984 almost exactly half of all the 7.5 m. women employed in the service sector were part-timers, and almost 45 per cent of all working women were employed on a part-time basis.

The first half of the 1980s in general, therefore, witnessed an extension of the basic long-term post-war trends in the composition of employment. The shift from manufacturing to services gathered pace and this was associated with a change in the composition of employment away from full-time male employment towards part-time female employment. This is not just a feature of recession. The increase in the total number employed from mid-1983 to mid-1984 was 389,000. Most of this was accounted for by an increase of 273,000 in the self-employed (which was heavily concentrated in the service sector and may or may not indicate the entrepreneurial flowering). Of the employees in employment there was an actual decline of 94,000 men offset by a total increase of 206,000 women. But the increase in part-time female employment was greater than this at 214,000, suggesting a decline in full-time employment for women. (*Employment Gazette*, March 1985, pp. 115, 117). There has been a continuation of the secular change in the identity of the typical wage earner and in the sources of (as it used to be thought) his wages. This is not just a feature of recession because the pattern continues in 'recovery'.

In the last section of this chapter we want to tackle the issue of why this change is a problem. The salient changes in the *composition* of employment since 1950 have been the relative and absolute decline of manufacturing employment and the increased significance of service employment. The employment changes reflect a decline of manufacturing which does create macro-economic problems. Manufacturing is a source of exports (and/or import substitutes) and these have become particularly crucial with the novel (post-1982) emergence of a trade deficit in manufactures and its extraordinarily rapid growth since 1983. This, however, is an issue which will be taken up more fully in the next chapter.

If we are concerned with employment effects, we must concede that, in the abstract, a service job is as good as a manufacturing job. In this light arguments bewailing the decline of manufacturing employment today might seem equivalent to bemoaning the displacement of agricultural employment by manufacturing employment in the process of industrialisation. But while manufacturing jobs in the industrial revolution usually offered better pay and conditions than agricultural jobs, service jobs now frequently offer inferior pay and conditions. Service jobs are not as good as manufacturing jobs for a variety of reasons. To begin with, part-time work plays a much greater role in the service sector than in manufacturing. For example, the Census of Employment for 1981 showed that 7.6 per cent of jobs in manufacturing were part-time as against 29.7 per cent in services. Moreover, the role of part-time work in services has been, and is, growing increasingly important: the 1971 Census of Employment showed part-time employment as only 23.5 per cent of service employment. So, the loss of a job in manufacturing is likely to be a full-time job: where a service job *is* available it is more likely to be part-time. In this sense the service job is unlikely to replace the income foregone by the loss of a manufacturing job.

This is also true for another reason. As we have already seen, the group most affected by the decline of manufacturing employment has been male manual workers. The absolute job loss has been much greater amongst men than amongst women because, despite a proportionately greater rate of decline in manufacturing employment for women, men make up a larger percentage of the total workforce. Equally the job loss has been greatest for manual workers and less marked for clerical and technical personnel. It is difficult for a displaced manual worker in manufacturing to obtain full-time employment in the service sector. Even if such full-time work can be found it is likely to be at markedly lower wages. As Table 3.15 shows, full-time manual workers' earnings in the personal service jobs are some 25–30 per cent below the level for manual workers in manufacturing employment. There is still a considerable gap even if we compare the semi-skilled manufacturing jobs (painting, repetitive assembly, etc.) where overall average earnings are nearly 20 per cent in excess of earnings in personal service jobs. Wage levels are, it is true, much

Table 3.15 Average gross weekly earnings for male manual workers by occupation, 1984

Occupation group	Per cent of sample	Earnings in £ per week
Catering, cleaning, hairdressing and other personal services	6.94	124.1
Materials processing (excluding metals)	5.09	155.0
Making and repairing (excluding metals and electrical)	8.74	154.9
Processing, making, repairing and related (metal and electrical)	31.56	165.6
Painting, repetitive assembling, production inspection, packaging and related	7.22	147.9
Construction, mining, etc.	8.35	154.1
Transport, materials moving and storing	19.7	151.6

Source: New Earnings Survey 1984

more nearly comparable in the productive service sector (construction and transport) but these parts of the service sector have been, like manufacturing, subject to contraction in employment. So, the decline of manufacturing employment *is* problematic because manufacturing offered working-class men the opportunity of, at least, relatively high manual earnings and full-time work. Of course, the service sector does offer a number of highly paid jobs in management and professional occupations. However, clearly these are not options which can be pursued by displaced manual workers from the manufacturing sector. The service sector, when it offers anything, generally offers low wages.

The decline of manufacturing employment and its effects on male manual employment thus clearly operates to affect the incomes of family units headed by male manual workers if they are the only wage earners in the family. However, if we jettison the Beveridge assumption of a labour force without married women then it might appear that the loss could, at least, be mitigated by the earnings of the displaced male worker's wife. In this sense, is it possible that the expansion of participation rates amongst married women blunts the edge of mass unemployment? The most systematic attempt to look at this issue is contained in a DHSS cohort study of 2,300 men who became unemployed in the autumn of 1978 (Moylan, Millar and Davies, 1984).

For the wife's earnings to mitigate the effects of unemployment we would need an increase in employment rates amongst the wives of unemployed men. In fact the cohort study reveals that the pattern is the opposite. As Table 3.16 shows, there was a net increase in employ-

Table 3.16 Changes in wives' employment status between registration and second interview by husbands' employment history between registration and second interview (DHSS cohort study 1978–9, in percentages

	Husbands' employment history since registration	
	Unemployed up to date of interview	*In full-time work at interview*
Wives not in work before registration	72	65
Proportion of these wives who started work	6	17
Wives in work before registration	26	34
Proportion of these wives who stopped work	20	9
Wives in work before registration and at second interview	21	31
Proportion of these wives whose:		
hours reduced by more than five	8	1
hours increased by more than five	1	8

Source: Moylan *et al.,* 1984

ment in the case of wives whose husbands had found full-time work between registration and the second interview; and there was a net decrease in employment for the wives of husbands who had remained unemployed. The decrease in economic activity was most marked amongst wives of supplementary benefit claimants. Moreover these results could not be explained by differences in family circumstances (age of youngest child and whether the child was of school age) (Moylan *et al.*, 1984, Tables 10, 13). Thus, far from a wife's earnings operating to mitigate the effects of male unemployment, loss of a wife's earnings is likely to exacerbate the effects of male unemployment and inequalities in family income are thereby increased. This result is largely explained by the way the social security system operates. At the time of the Moylan study an unemployed male claimant of *unemployment benefit* was entitled to an adult dependant's allowance of £9.75 per week, claimable if the man's wife did not work or if her net earnings were less than the dependant's allowance. If the wife's net earnings exceeded this level then the adult dependant's allowance was taken away. In the case of the unemployed male claimant on *supplementary benefit*, however, a more strict earnings rule applied. If the wife was working she was allowed up to £4 net earnings. Above that level benefit was reduced pound for pound. The contrast still remains and has been intensified because the relative position of the supplementary benefit claimant has further deteriorated: in November 1984 the adult dependant allowance was £17.55 while the £4 rule for supplementary benefit remains unchanged.

The changes in both the composition and the level of employment have thus severely hit significant groups. In particular the working-class two-parent family has suffered from the collapse of the relatively high-wage manufacturing sector. The loss of husband's income due, usually, to loss of a manufacturing job could (because of the effects of low wages and part-time work) at best have only been mitigated by his wife's earnings. However, even this meagre palliative is ineffective since female participation and employment rates are consistently lower where the husband is unemployed.

Nonetheless, as we have seen, one of the outstanding trends in the post-war labour market has been the growth in women's employment which almost entirely accounts for the increase in the labour force. Surely this has progressive distributional effects even though it does not look after two-parent families. Does this contradiction of one of Beveridge's basic assumptions represent the one bright spot in the UK labour market? One favourable pointer would seem to be that registered female unemployment at 9.6 per cent in June 1985 was significantly lower than registered male unemployment rates at 15.7 per cent. But this contrast overstates the extent of the gap: available evidence strongly suggests that unregistered unemployment is much

Occupational group	Industry Group								
	Food, drink, tobacco	Textiles, clothing, footwear	Manufacturing[1]	Distribution	Professional and scientific services	Insurance, banking and public administration	Other services	Primary industry	All working women
	%	%	%	%	%	%	%	%	%
Professional	—	—	1	1	2	0	0	—	1
Teaching	—	—	—	—	22	0	0	—	6
Nursing, medical and social	—	—	—	—	23	1	2	—	7
Other intermediate non-manual	2	2	8	13	1	8	6	19	6
Clerical	26	14	36	22	19	73	27	21	30
Sales	3	—	1	49	0	1	2	—	9
Skilled manual	8	21	19	3	5	2	10	—	7
Semi-skilled factory	50	55	30	3	0	0	2	6	10
Semi-skilled domestic	2	1	1	1	14	2	33	2	11
Other semi-skilled	—	5	1	5	2	1	6	52	4
Unskilled	9	2	3	3	12	12	12	—	9

Occupational group and social class of full- and part-time working women

Occupational group	Social class	Full-time	Part-time	All working women
		%	%	%
Professional	I	1	1	1
Teaching	II	8 ⎫	3 ⎫	6 ⎫
Nursing, medical and social		7 ⎬ 24	6 ⎬ 12	7 ⎬ 19
Other intermediate non-manual		9 ⎭	3 ⎭	6 ⎭
Clerical	III non-manual	39	20	30
Sales		6	12	9
Skilled manual	III manual	8	6	7
Semi-skilled factory	IV	13 ⎫	7 ⎫	10 ⎫
Semi-skilled domestic		4 ⎬ 20	20 ⎬ 32	11 ⎬ 25
Other semi-skilled		3 ⎭	5 ⎭	4 ⎭
Unskilled	V	2	17	9

[1] Other than engineering and metal manufacture
Source: Based on J. Martin and C. Roberts, *Women and Employment: A Lifetime Perspective*, Social Survey Report 1143, 1984, Tables 3.2 and 3.5

more prevalent amongst women. For example, the 1983 Labour Force Survey revealed a figure of 600,000 non-claimant unemployed of which 430,000 were women. Adjusting the male and female unemployment rates to take account of the unregistered unemployed would mean that the gap between male and female unemployment rates would fall from 6 to roughly 3 per cent.

More pertinently, if the post-war period has been one which has witnessed a quantitative expansion in women's employment opportunities, qualitatively there has been little change. A recent extensive survey based on an unusually large sample showed that only in one industrial sector (professional and scientific services) did a substantial proportion of the women employed fill one of the higher occupational groups – and that exception was accounted for by teachers and nurses, who are not at the top end of the professional categories (Martin and Roberts, 1984). In manufacturing about three-quarters of the women fell into two occupations (clerical and semi-skilled factory), whilst in the growing and prosperous sector of insurance, banking and public administration three-quarters of the women employed fell into a single occupational group (clerical) (see Table 3.17). The broad picture is confirmed by looking at the proportion of women employed in high-status occupations. Comparisons made over a very long time-scale during which many influences (including two world wars) are supposed to have revolutionised the place of women in the economy and society show remarkably little change in this respect until very recent times (Table 3.18). In 1961 women accounted for only 8 per cent of the administrative civil service, 9 per cent of dentists, 5 per cent of barristers, 2 per cent of solicitors but almost one-quarter of the medical practitioners in England and Wales. Of the 250,000 economically

Table 3.18   Women's share of top jobs

Per cent of women among total in each group	1911	1971	1981
Doctors	2	20	31.7
Accountants	0.2	3	10.3
Architects and town planners	0.08	5	8.0
Judges, barristers and solicitors	0	6	17.6
Ministers, MPs and senior government[1]	5	12	23.4[2]
Local authority senior officers[1]	5	15	47.1[3]

[1] These two groups were not precisely defined in the 1911 occupational classification and included officers below the senior grades.
[2] 1981 figures relates to 'General Administrators – national government' (HEO and above). For Assistant Secretary and above the percentage was 5.4.
[3] 1981 relates to 'Local Government (administrative and executive)'.
Source: C. Hakin, 1979, p. 34, and 1981 Census, vol. on *Economic Activity*.

active people in Great Britain with technical and scientific quali-
fications only 18,000 were women: the comparable figures for managers were 360,000 and 18,000 (Roberts and Smith, 1966, p. 99).
Only as general practitioners did women make early and substantial
progress towards claiming a share of high-status jobs which was
anything like their overall share in the total labour force.

The low status and earnings of women's work has been reinforced
by the growing proportion of women who are in part-time employment. The Martin and Roberts survey demonstrated that part-time
women workers were concentrated even more heavily into the service
sectors than were their full-time sisters: (82 per cent of part-time
women were employed in service industries and 15 per cent in manufacture, compared to 72 per cent and 27 per cent of full-time women
workers (Martin and Roberts, 1984, Table 3.4)). Within the service
sector, part-time women are more likely to be employed in lower
grades (Tables 3.17 and 3.19) since the distribution of part-time
women by both social class and occupational order clearly slips down
a notch when compared with the extremely modest heights reached
by their full-time sisters. This is strongly related to the disrupted

Table 3.19 Occupational order for jobs of full- and part-time working
women

Occupational order	Full-time	Part-time
	%	%
Managerial general	—	—
Professionals supporting management	2	0
Professionals in health, education and welfare	16	10
Literary, artistic and sports	1	1
Professionals in engineering and science	1	0
Other managerial	5	1
Clerical	41	22
Selling	6	13
Security	0	0
Catering, cleaning and hairdressing	10	41
Farming and fishing	1	2
Material processing (excluding metal)	1	1
Making and repairing (excluding metal)	6	4
Metal processing, making, repairing	3	1
Painting, assembling, packing	6	3
Construction and mining	0	—
Transport	1	1
Miscellaneous	0	0
	100	100
Base	1,877	1,477

Source: Martin and Roberts, 1984, Table 3.3

nature of the lifetime work cycle of most women. The pattern 'changes from being full-time before childbirth to a mixture of part-time and full-time after the first child. Approximately two-thirds of women's first return to work is to a part-time job and there is much downward occupational mobility at this point' (Dex, 1984, p. 1). It is not surprising, therefore, to find that the average amount of time spent working part-time increases with age (Dex, 1984, p. 4).

Women's earnings are, and have always been, lower than those of men. In 1886 three-quarters of all women workers received less than 15 shillings (75p) a week, but only one man in forty was paid so little, whilst 96 per cent of men (but only 5 per cent of women) earned more than £1 a week. In 1906 the only broad industrial group where full-time women earned on average more than half the average male earnings was textiles (55 per cent) (*British Labour Statistics, Historical Abstract*, 1971). Table 3.20 sets out the post-war situation as far as full-time manual workers are concerned. Average weekly earnings for women are three-fifths those of men; average hourly earnings about two-thirds. Most of the gains were made in the 1970s, assisted by legislation on sex discrimination, but there is some evidence that – in the crucial area of hourly rates – some of the advances were eroded after the mid-1970s (see, for example, Table 3.21 based on the 1983 National Expenditure Survey).

Lower earnings for women is hardly news (though this should not obscure its significance). It is of interest, however, to set variations in the average levels of earnings in different sectors of the economy against the composition of female employment. Table 3.22 shows two very broad aspects of this. First, women's pay (both in absolute terms and relative to that of men) was generally significantly higher in the public sector than in the private sector. Second, in the industries where much female employment was concentrated – especially distribution and catering – women's earnings were especially low. The importance of these findings is re-emphasised by recent employment trends. In the 1970s a great deal of the extra employment for women was in the, relatively, better-paid public sector: in the 1980s employment here has declined and most of the opportunities for women's employment were concentrated in the low-wage private sector.

There is the further fact that much of the 1980s employment for women was, as we have seen, for part-time working. It is thus pertinent to notice that the trend in relative rates of pay for part-time female workers is downward. Table 3.23 indicates that female part-time rates compared to female full-time rates fell from 99 to 89 per cent between 1947 and 1981; and after first rising has tended to fall away (from 65 to 61 per cent) as a proportion of full-time male rates since 1977.

Finally, there is the problem of single-parent families, over 90 per cent of which have a woman as head. Here, a woman's earnings

Table 3.20 Average earnings and hours, manual workers, for full-time adults, men and women, 1948–1984

Year	Industry group	Average weekly earnings			Hours		Average hourly earnings		
		M	F	F as % of M	M	F	M	F	F as % of M
		s d	s d				d	d	
1948	Manufacturing	138 8	73 4	52.9	46.5	41.4	35.9	21.2	59.1
	All industries	134 0	72 11		46.7	41.4	34.6	21.1	
1958	Manufacturing	265 5	134 1	50.5	47.3	40.9	67.3	39.3	58.4
	All industries	258 8	134 1		47.7	41.0	64.6	39.2	
1968	Manufacturing	472 4	226 3	47.9	45.8	38.2	123.8	71.1	57.3
	All industries	459 11	225 11		46.4	38.3	118.9	70.8	
		£	£				p	p	
1978	Manufacturing	84.77	50.08	59.1	43.5	37.2	194.9	134.6	69.1
	All industries	83.50	50.03		44.2	37.4	189.9	133.8	
1984	Manufacturing	158.9	96.0	60.4	44.4	39.9	358.1	238.1	66.5
	All industries	152.7	93.5		44.3	39.4	345.0	238.0	

Sources: *British Labour Statistics Historical Abstract*, 1971, Tables 47–9 for 1948–68; *Employment Gazette*, December 1983 for 1978 and March 1985 for 1984

Table 3.21 Women's earnings as percentage of men's, 1970–1983 (average gross hourly earnings, excluding overtime, full-time employees)

1970	63.1	1978	73.9	1982	73.9
1975	72.1	1979	73.0	1983	74.2
1976	75.1	1980	73.5		
1977	75.5	1981	74.8		

are of more basic importance to the household's domestic economy because they do not represent a second income. A significant minority of families (one in eight) in 1982–4 are now single-parent families (Office of Population Censuses and Surveys, 1985, Monitor CHS/1) and 5 per cent of the population were living in such families in 1983 (*Social Trends*, 16, 1986).

There is some evidence to suggest that, even relative to overall female wage rates, female heads of one-parent families are a relatively low-paid group with relatively low activity rates (Popay, Rimmer and Rossiter, 1982). Again much of the explanation lies within the social security system. Widowed mothers, for example, received (November 1984) a (taxable) allowance of £35.80 together with a (non-taxable) child dependant allowance of £7.65 per week. These are not subject to any earnings limits. In contrast, separated or single parents in receipt of supplementary benefit are allowed to earn only £4 without loss of benefit, lose half of anything earned between £4 and £20, after which benefit is cut pound for pound. As a result many more widowed mothers take up part-time employment (often the most convenient form of work for lone mothers with young children), whilst for single parents, to make it worthwhile working at all it is necessary to work full-time (National Consumer Council, 1984, pp. 103–4, 108–9).

The conclusion must be that in many fundamental respects the presuppositions of the Keynes-Beveridge approach did not materialise in the post-war British experience. This is so despite the fact that Keynes's fundamental objective was realised in the long post-war continuance of full employment. That was an important gain and a major opportunity. It seems, however, to owe little to the kind of demand management or investment intervention proposed in the *General Theory* (though this now entrenched view may unduly discount the psychological effects on business confidence). More pertinently, any Keynesian reflation would now have to confront (besides the range of external and micro problems considered in the next chapter) an employment difficulty Keynes had not anticipated. When Keynes argued for demand management to control employment he was concerned only with the level of employment and implicitly assumed this

Table 3.22 Average weekly earnings, men and women, by sectors and industries, April 1980

| | | Men | | Women | | | |
		Manual	Non-manual	Manual	Per cent of men	Non-manual	Per cent of men
All sectors:							
Average gross weekly earnings, £s		111.7	143.3	68.0	60.9	82.7	57.7
Average gross hourly earnings, p		245.8	360.8	172.1	70.0	221.2	61.3
Average weekly hours		45.4	38.7	39.6		36.7	
Average gross weekly earnings, £							
Public sector:							
Public services							
Central government	Weekly £	114.6	143.0	71.4	62.3	92.8	64.9
	Hourly p	102.1	142.3	68.2	66.8	93.9	65.9
Local government	Weekly £	104.6	151.6	72.1	68.9	89.1	58.8
	Hourly p	100.7	137.6	65.0	64.5	98.9	71.9
Public corporations	Weekly £	122.1	144.7	89.9	73.6	85.3	58.9
	Hourly p	110.3	140.2	66.6	60.4	72.8	51.9
Private sector:							
Food, drink and tobacco	Weekly £	116.0	142.5	70.7		78.6	
	Hourly p	232.5	368.1	170.4	73.3	211.0	57.3
Distributive trades	Weekly £	96.0	121.2	61.8		65.0	
	Hourly p	207.6	301.6	157.4	75.8	169.1	56.1
Professional and scientific	Weekly £	100.0	137.5	65.1		93.7	
	Hourly p	205.7	388.9	170.9	83.1	257.8	66.3
Insurance, banking and finance	Weekly £	106.6	158.2	—		79.0	
	Hourly p	231.7	424.7	—		217.9	51.3
Catering	Weekly £	78.6	126.2	60.7		81.3	
	Hourly p	175.2	312.4	153.7	87.7	214.2	68.6

Source: New Earnings Survey (1980), Part A

Table 3.23 Mean average gross hourly earnings of part-time females, full-time females and full-time males in manual occupations, all industries, Great Britain, April 1947–April 1981

| | Relative hourly earnings | |
April	Part-time female as % of full-time females	Part-time female as % of full-time males
1947	99.0	60.3
1952	97.0	59.8
1957	94.5	57.9
1962	94.1	56.4
1967	93.3	55.8
1975	93.9	62.7
1977	92.0	65.4
1980	89.4	62.6
1981	89.2	61.5

Source: Robinson, O. and Wallace J., Department of Employment research paper no. 43, 1984, Table 3

would solve the social problem. This is, however, far from certain if any increase in activity simply sucks in more lower-paid part-time female workers. Post-war full employment also met Beveridge's most crucial explicit assumption. None the less his design for social welfare foundered well before the full employment underpinning was removed. Some of the reasons for this have already been explored in chapter 2 on occupational welfare: as this chapter shows, another reason was the falsification of his assumptions about the composition of employment. The shift from full-time, well-paid, male manual employment in manufacturing to part-time, low-paid, female employment in services could not be contained within the Beveridge framework.

4 New terrains of policy

The previous two chapters have reviewed some of the major economic and social changes in post-war Britain and have established the failure of liberal collectivism in that context. In the sphere of social policy, liberal collectivism offered a state minimum, leaving provision above the minimum to an independent private sector. Welfare provision became increasingly tied to occupational position and, with the benefit of extravagant state subsidy, the complex panoply of benefits had a strongly regressive effect. In the sphere of employment, liberal collectivism offered full employment at wages broadly adequate for subsistence without a second income. More and more during the 1970s and 1980s this outcome has not been maintained and there has been a major deterioration in the level and composition of employment. In this chapter, we aim to explain why this failure constitutes a crisis and what has been and could be done to solve it by introducing and defending policies and programmes which go beyond those envisaged by liberal collectivists like Keynes and Beveridge.

(1) The foreign trade crisis

All the commentators who discuss a 'British disease' accept that, at least in economic terms, things are bad and likely to get worse. What other conclusion is possible when unemployment has risen to a level of over 13 per cent? The more scholarly commentators debate the declines of manufacturing output and employment which have not been reversed by 'economic recovery' although the position is different in other advanced industrial countries as dissimilar as Japan and the United States. Unemployment obviously does create a distributional problem. On the other hand the vast majority are in employment and the many beneficiaries of fiscal and occupational welfare are doing nicely. In this situation many quite understandably do not see why our slow national decline of the past forty years cannot continue in a way which is tolerably comfortable for the majority of our citizens. Against such complacency, we would wish to argue that we are now caught in what Smith (1984) has correctly identified as a new and threatening 'British economic crisis'. This national crisis is motored by the uncontrolled decline of manufacturing as an economic activity and will be manifest before the end of the 1980s in the form of severe balance of payments deficits. Massive trade deficits in the later stages of deindustrialisation are a problem because (within an orthodox liberal collectivist policy framework) they can only be controlled at the expense of a substantial general decline in living standards. This outcome is inevitable if the orthodox policy solution of deflation and monetary squeeze is applied to deal with chronic payments problems in a country which starts from an unemployment rate over 13 per cent and in a world where improved price competitiveness does not sell poor quality manufactures. On this scenario, Britain at the end of the 1980s would become the first advanced industrial country to get the sharp deflationary shock treatment which the IMF has traditionally reserved for deficit-running primary producers in Africa and Latin America. Under these admittedly very different conditions, deflation not only cuts living standards but also undermines the political liberty and stability which the liberal collectivists cherish.

The economics of liberal collectivism were of course formulated in a more optimistic context where it was assumed either that foreign trade did not exist or that foreign trade would not be a problem. The summary recapitulation of Keynes's theory, in chapter 18 of the *General Theory* (hereafter *GT*), simply assumes a closed economy. The earlier discussion of the multiplier effects of increased investment did recognise the possibility that injected expenditures might leak abroad:

> In an open system with foreign-trade relations some part of the multiplier of the increased investment will accrue to the benefit of employment in foreign countries since a proportion of the increased consumption will diminish our own country's favourable foreign balance; so that if we consider only the effect on domestic employment as distinct from world employment, we must diminish the full figure of the multiplier. (Keynes, *GT*, p. 120)

Keynes clearly assumed that this kind of leakage of purchasing power would not in practice be a problem. In taking this position, Keynes was only following the lead set by Kahn when he introduced the concept of the multiplier in a famous 1931 *Economic Journal* article. Kahn recognised that increased expenditure on public works would only have beneficial effects if certain conditions were satisfied. These specifically included the conditions that 'a man who becomes employed devotes a large proportion of the increase in his income to home-produced consumption goods' and 'increased production necessitates the import of only a small proportion of raw materials'.

But the point of Kahn's subsequent argument is that both these conditions were likely to be met in Britain in the 1930s and therefore a public works programme of road building would have large multiplied beneficial effects.

If the liberal collectivists believed that foreign trade was not a problem or indeed was a theoretical complication which could often be assumed away, they did not believe in autarchy as a desirable goal. As we shall see later, Keynes in the 1930s sanctioned protection when free trade proved damaging to the national interest; he was never an enthusiast for free capital movement and by the 1940s he was concerned with the creation of international institutions which would not leave the burden of adjustment to be borne by debtor countries. But, at the same time, Keynes believed that (with suitable institutions and safeguards) a liberal international regime of free trade and stable exchange rates would be generally beneficent for all trading nations. This conclusion has to be set in the context of the universal assumption of the 1930s that the major axis of trade exchange would be between developed and less developed countries. Britain would naturally play a major role in this kind of trade system as a specialist exporter of manufactures and an importer of foodstuffs and raw materials. In this case, according to the theory of comparative advantage, foreign trade should improve world prosperity and, as we shall argue later, the possibility that such trade might compromise domestic prosperity does not really exist. All this helps explain why Keynes involved himself in wartime attempts to reconstruct the post-war international economic system under a liberal basis.

Within the liberal economic order which Bretton Woods created, the expected and the unexpected happened. The importance of foreign trade to the advanced economies predictably increased; as Table 4.1 shows, despite significant national differences import penetration and export sales increased in all the advanced industrial countries, especially after 1965. More surprisingly, trade amongst the advanced industrial countries boomed as there was a huge expansion in the interchange of finished manufactures between such countries. In 1963–73, for example, manufacturing trade within the developed world grew at an annual rate of 12 per cent which was nearly twice as fast as trade between the developed and the developing world (Piore and Sabell, 1984, p. 186). As a result of this secular increase, by 1973 70 per cent of North American exports went to the industrial world as did 78 per cent of West European and 46 per cent of Japanese exports (Piore and Sabell, 1984, p. 188).

The old system, under which each major industrial country at least supplied the bulk of its own consumer and producer goods, was transformed throughout the 1960s and 1970s. The results were most visible and dramatic in Western European countries whose car parks

Table 4.1   Exports and imports as percentage of GNP

	1950	1955	1960	1965	1970	1975	1980
	Exports of goods/services as percentage of GNP						
USA	4.9	5.0	5.5	5.7	6.4	9.6	12.9
Japan	12.5	11.0	11.5	11.0	11.0	13.5	15.0
Germany	11.0	20.0	20.0	19.0	22.0	26.0	28.5
France	16.0	15.0	14.0	12.5	15.0	18.5	21.0
UK	22.0	21.5	20.0	18.5	22.0	25.5	28.0
Italy	12.0	11.0	13.0	15.0	17.0	21.0	23.0
	Imports of goods/services as percentage of GNP						
USA	4.2	4.5	4.6	4.7	6.0	8.3	12.0
Japan	11.5	10.5	11.0	10.0	10.0	14.0	16.0
Germany	13.0	17.5	17.0	19.0	20.0	23.5	29.0
France	15.0	13.0	11.0	11.5	15.0	18.0	21.0
UK	23.0	23.0	21.5	19.5	21.5	27.5	26.0
Italy	13.0	12.0	15.0	14.0	18.0	22.0	27.0

Source: Piore and Sabell (1984, p. 185)

and shops of the 1950s were dominated by indigenous manufacturers. Twenty years later imports from nearby West European countries were everywhere and in consumer durables, like cars, the normal import share was around 30 per cent. Much of this trade was between more or less adjacent countries; in 1973 70 per cent of French exports were sold in markets within a 1500 kilometre radius of Paris (Piore and Sabell, 1984, p. 236). But contiguity was not everything because the new trade in manufactures amongst advanced countries was in differentiated consumer and producer goods where packaging and performance were important. In this situation, there were significant national differences in the capacity of different advanced economies to organise production of high-quality manufactures whose non-price characteristics made them attractive to domestic and foreign buyers. The Japanese came from nowhere and ended up in a league of their own in car and consumer electronics production. The Europeans figured in league division two with the Germans at the top and the British at the bottom of the table of manufacturing capability.

With Britain increasingly integrated into an open international economy of competing industrial countries, the repercussions of inferiority were quite dramatic. As in other advanced industrial countries, the share of British manufacturing output which was exported increased steadily from 20 per cent or less in the period 1955–60 to just under 33 per cent by the early 1980s (Williams, Williams and Thomas, 1983, pp. 118–19). This was hardly cause for congratulation because it meant the British were increasingly committed to an economic activity where they were at a comparative disadvantage. The

Table 4.2 UK balance of payments in finished manufactured goods, 1964–
1984, £m.

1964	1,751	1971	2,333	1978	3,745
1965	1,969	1972	1,675	1979	1,964
1966	2,042	1973	1,205	1980	4,002
1967	1,619	1974	2,022	1981	3,083
1968	1,732	1975	3,241	1982	1,285
1969	1,949	1976	3,935	1983	−2,501
1970	2,103	1977	4,256	1984	−3,647

Source: UK Balance of Payments, Annual CSO

decline in our share of world trade in manufactures is the best single
measure of British inferiority in this trade; over the past thirty years
it has declined from over 20 per cent to well under 10 per cent
(Williams *et al.*, 1983). In this situation the British could not really
afford their high and growing propensity to import finished manufactures which were supplying 30 per cent of home demand by 1980,
although they had supplied less than 10 per cent of home demand
through the 1950s (Williams *et al.*, 1983, pp. 118–19). All this was
reflected in a dramatic turn-round in the balance between the value
of imported and exported manufactures. Back in the early 1950s, the
value of British manufactured exports was up to three times as large
as the value of our manufactured imports and in the early 1960s the
value of our manufactured exports was up to twice as large as the
value of our manufactured imports (Williams *et al.*, 1983, pp. 118–
19). But as Table 4.2 and Figure 4.1 show, the pattern since has been
one of unsteady but sustained deterioration in the ratio of manufactured exports to imports. Despite this trend, the positive balance
in the trade in manufactures held up in the 1960s and 1970s; as Table
4.2 shows, the surplus was always over £1.5 billion and the largest
surplus in nominal money terms of £4.3 billion was achieved as
recently as 1977. But since 1980 there has been a very rapid deterioration with the first negative balance recorded in 1983 and a deficit
of nearly £4 billion in 1984.

At the same time, the overall balance of payments in the early
1980s has been in healthy surplus. It has always been the case that
surpluses in some items on the current account have covered deficits
in others. But as Figure 4.2 shows the pattern of surpluses and deficits
has changed dramatically and ominously over the past two decades.
In the early 1960s the characteristic pattern was that the deficits were
being covered by a very large surplus on manufactures and by a
substantial surplus on interest, profit and dividends which was about
one-fifth of that on manufactures. Against these surpluses were the
main deficit categories of food, raw materials and fuel in that order.
In effect, surpluses on manufactures and overseas investment paid for

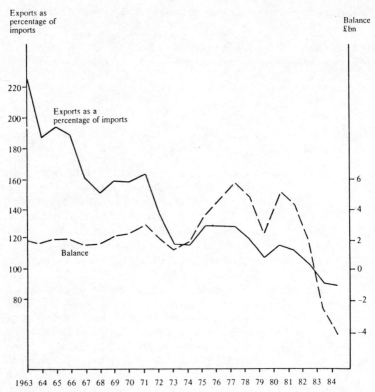

Exports as
percentage of
imports

Balance
£bn

Source: House of Lords Select Committee on Overseas Trade, 1985, p. 8

Figure 4.1   UK balance of trade in manufactured goods, 1963–1984

deficits in all other areas. By 1983 the pattern had radically shifted. Interest, profit and dividends remained a healthy source of surplus but the major surplus areas were now fuel (oil) and services which had been in deficit previously. Over half the total surplus of 1983 came from oil whose balance of trade was in surplus to the extent of £6.2 billion. On the deficit side in 1983, food remained the largest single deficit item but relatively it accounted for a smaller proportion of the total deficit because significant savings on foodstuff imports have been achieved as a result of the extravagant subsidy of domestic agriculture under the Common Agricultural Policy. In view of our early and complete industrialisation, it is ironic that agriculture should now be the only industry where import penetration has been contained and self-sufficiency increased over the past decade. In manufacturing the trend has been quite different and, as a result, manufacturing is now a major deficit item. From this analysis of sectorial surpluses and

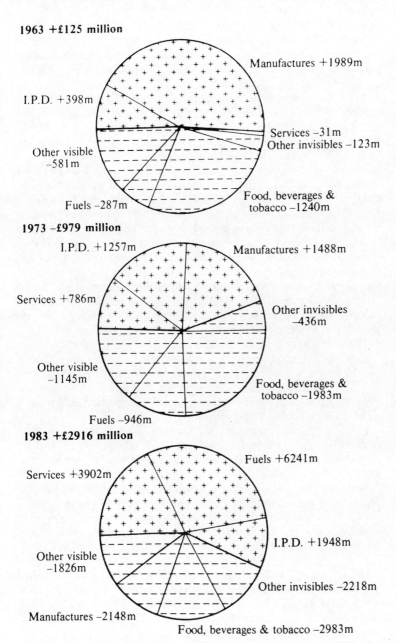

1963 +£125 million

Manufactures +1989m

I.P.D. +398m

Services −31m
Other invisibles −123m

Other visible −581m

Fuels −287m

Food, beverages & tobacco −1240m

1973 −£979 million

I.P.D. +1257m

Manufactures +1488m

Services +786m

Other invisibles −436m

Other visible −1145m

Food, beverages & tobacco −1983m

Fuels −946m

1983 +£2916 million

Fuels +6241m

Services +3902m

I.P.D. +1948m

Other visible −1826m

Other invisibles −2218m

Manufactures −2148m

Food, beverages & tobacco −2983m

Source: Lords Select Committee on Overseas Trade, Department of Trade Memorandum, 1985, p. 25

Figure 4.2 Breakdown of current account surpluses and deficits

deficits, the problem emerges clearly enough. The trade account depends on North Sea oil which is a depleting asset and manufacturing trade has become a rapidly increasing deficit item. How then is the current account to be balanced in future without a sharp cutback in living standards?

It is clear that a crisis will come when the oil runs out but how quickly will it run out? Before we turn to that issue it is worth reviewing how Britain has become a major oil producer and exporter in the past ten years. The first North Sea oil came ashore in 1975 and in that year we produced just 1.6 million tonnes. In 1985 we will produce about 135 million tonnes and that makes Britain the world's fourth largest oil producer, producing more oil than Saudi Arabia. Production has built up rapidly and will decline after 1985 because the government has adopted an extravagant depletion policy of pumping out as much oil as quickly as possible from limited reserves. Currently, Britain is a major oil exporter and produces 80 per cent more oil than is needed for domestic consumption. At the current rate, proven and probable reserves in the North Sea will only last for another ten years. Successive Labour and Tory governments have behaved like foolish virgins. Profligate depletion policies yield larger tax revenues and payments advantages in the short run; but they also bring closer the prospect of a sharp, painful adjustment when the oil runs out.

It is not easy to be certain or precise about when this will happen. We know that production from existing fields (on stream or under development) will fall away very rapidly; by the mid-1990s production from existing fields will supply only half of projected UK demand. What happens then depends on production from unexploited reserves most of which are in smaller oilfields in deep water. The oil companies are probably underestimating the volume of oil in these new fields but that is only prudent because there is substantial uncertainty about how much oil can be recovered from the more inaccessible and geologically difficult fields. The amount of oil that is recovered will depend on the price of oil and advances in oil-drilling techniques. Apart from the uncertainty about how much oil will be supplied in the medium term, there is further uncertainty about domestic demand which is currently flat and running around 70 million tonnes of oil per annum. Most estimates show demand flat till the end of the century (e.g. Esso, 1984). But there is substantial scope for reducing demand through energy conservation measures because the British are extravagant users of energy by the standards of other advanced countries. UK energy consumption per unit of GDP is the highest in the European community; it is over 30 per cent higher than the community average (NEDO, 1984, p. 8).

It is against this background of uncertainty that we have to view the official estimates of North Sea oil production till 1989 (See

Table 4.3   Official estimates of North Sea oil production

1985	120–135 million tonnes oil equivalent
1986	110–130
1987	95–125
1988	85–120
1989	80–115

Source: Lords Select Committee on Overseas Trade, Report, 1985, p. 40

Table 4.3). The government prudently refuses to estimate production beyond 1989 and the estimate of production in five years' time is clearly labelled as a guess because it includes an error margin of plus or minus 20 per cent around the central estimate. It is certain that oil production will decline much more slowly than it built up. The official estimates suggest that North Sea oil output will decline at a rate of 5 per cent per annum from the production peak in 1985. If this annual rate of decline sounds fairly modest, it should be remembered that it is a 5 per cent *compound* loss. The cumulative effect of modest annual reductions will be quite marked. Certainly, the effect on the payments situation, which is what primarily concerns us, will be dramatic. If the official projections are extrapolated then output will decline so that our current oil export surplus vanishes and we reach a point of self-sufficiency where North Sea oil just covers domestic consumption in the 1990s, maybe in the early or mid-1990s. Self-sufficiency sounds attractive and it is an energy privilege which the mainland European countries do not and will not enjoy. But in payments terms it is simply not enough for the British economy. Currently, in payments terms, our domestic consumption of North Sea oil saves us £15 billion which would otherwise have to be spent on importing oil; the official figures also show that our net oil exports (or the margin of production above domestic consumption) will in payments terms contribute some £7 billion in 1984 and £10 billion in 1985 (Keegan, 1985, p. 43). At the point of self-sufficiency in the 1990s the £7–10 billion cushion will be completely removed and the crisis must then be intense.

Our argument so far reinforces the prevailing notion that the crisis will happen when the oil runs out. In fact, we wish to argue strongly that the crisis will be upon us long before this happens some time in the 1990s. It is misleading to present the British problem as that of adjusting to the oil run-down. Before we have completely dissipated the unique advantage of North Sea oil we are going to suffer from the unique disadvantage of a rapidly increasing trade deficit in manufactures. As Table 4.4 indicates, Britain's position is unique amongst the major industrial countries. The USA, like Britain, does run a deficit on manufacturing trade but that is in entirely different circumstances and part of a remarkable recovery from economic

Table 4.4   Manufacturing trade balances ($m.)

	1978	1979	1980	1981	1982	1983
UK	858	514	719	524	91	−877
France	950	955	590	743	251	354
W. Germany	3911	4905	5160	5167	5590	5174
Japan	5272	5961	7852	9463	8579	8636
USA	388	706	1664	1076	−429	−1796

Source: Nedo, 1984, p. 14

recession. West Germany and Japan are actually increasing the size of their surpluses in current prices. Even a relatively unsuccessful West European manufacturing country like France has a healthy though declining manufacturing surplus.

What is really alarming about the British position is not so much the fact of deficit but the recent trend rate of increase in the manufacturing deficit. The balance of trade in manufactures was in surplus in 1982, and then went into deficit to the extent of £2.4 billion in 1983. This deficit increased to £3.8 billion in 1984 and will be larger again in 1985 because there was a deficit of £2 billion in the first half year (Lords Select Committee, Report, 2985, p. 40). If we extrapolate this trend rate of increase, we could expect the manufacturing deficit to increase by perhaps £1.5 billion or more per annum. Such an increase would create payments problems long before the oil runs down to the point of self-sufficiency some time in the 1990s. In this context, it is also worth observing that the recent escalating deficit is caused by a substantial increase in import volumes in a situation where British export volumes are static. Between 1980 and 1984 the volume of (non-oil) visible imports increased by nearly 30 per cent, while the volume of (non-oil) visible exports was fluctuating around and often below 1980 levels (*Economic Trends,* September 1985, p. 78). The alarming trend of manufactured import and export volumes is graphically illustrated in Figure 4.3. As we shall see later in this chapter, this causal mechanism provides us with some kind of clue to the new kinds of protectionist policy interventions which are necessary to deal with the coming crisis. More immediately, it also provides us with some indications of how and why the coming payments crisis will be different from those which occurred regularly, every five years or so, in Britain in the 1950s and 1960s.

Twenty years ago, the pattern was one of cyclical overheating at full employment and full capacity utilisation. Each of these episodes produced a once-and-for-all step-like increase in import penetration (Williams *et al.*, 1983, p. 8). In these 'crises' a modest damping down of demand and 2.5 per cent unemployment worked every time to stabilise import penetration. During the long boom before 1973 that

Graph 1   UK Exports of Manufactures

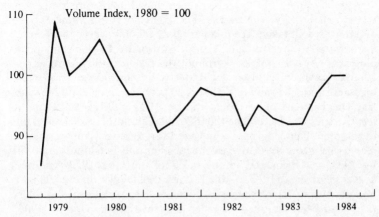

Graph 2   UK Imports of Manufactures

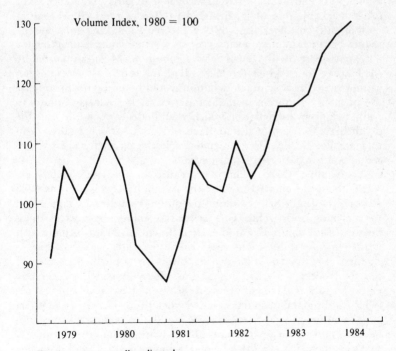

Figures are seasonally adjusted

Source: Lords Select Committee on Overseas Trade, Department of Trade
Memorandum, 1985, p. 22

Figure 4.3   UK manufactured export and import volumes

was quite enough to maintain the payments surplus on manufacturing trade because British manufacturers were finding it relatively easy to increase absolute export volumes (even though they were losing their relative share of world trade). The coming crisis will be entirely different. It will take place in a national economy where the demand for imports is already being damped down by 13 per cent unemployment. Against this background, the recent rapid rise of import volumes is a direct function of de-industrialisation and recession which together produced something like a 20 per cent destruction of manufacturing capacity in the four years after 1980 (Lords Select Committee, Evidence, 11 December 1984, Q.238). This process of contraction in the manufacturing base is not yet over. It is well known that, in real terms, gross fixed investment in plant and machinery had not, by 1985, yet recovered to the levels of the later 1970s (*Economic Trends*, September 1985, p. 18). It is less well known that in 1985, net manufacturing investment was negative because the rate at which plant had been scrapped exceeded new investment (Godley, 1986). In this situation, it is hardly surprising that manufacturing output and exports had by 1985 barely recovered to early 1980 levels. Nor is it remarkable that major firms, like ICI which lost 20 per cent of its domestic customer base during the recession, currently see the reduced British manufacturing base as an 'inadequate spring-board for export-led growth' (Lords Select Committee, Memo submitted by Mr Harvey-Jones, 14 March 1985). If all this is the case, the question cannot really be how much deflation would be necessary to stabilise the payments situation in the coming crisis. It is clearly lunatic to contemplate severe deflation which would effectively administer the death blow to a national manufacturing sector which is already in uncontrolled decline. Far better to avoid the payments crisis which requires the deflationary 'final solution'.

When active crisis prevention was called for, the Thatcher government stolidly attempted to deny the possibility of crisis. In its 1985 Report, the Lords Select Committee on Overseas Trade highlighted the alarming trade trends. Chancellor Lawson appeared as a witness before this committee and the Department of Trade submitted a written memorandum. The reassuring official line was that there is nothing to worry about for two reasons. First, a payments crisis will not come because market mechanisms, especially changes in the real exchange rate, will ensure automatic adjustment as the oil runs out. As a Bank of England official responded when pressed by the committee, 'what you describe as complacency, could also be described as confidence in the market mechanism' (Lords Select Committee, Evidence, 11 December 1984, Q.231). Second, a payments crisis will not come because the surplus on services will grow and the deficit on manufactures will be reduced as new industries and enterprises replace those we have lost in the past few years. As Chancellor Lawson argued, 'I think you will see the balance shifting with the older industrialised countries moving more into the service areas as the Newly Industrialised Countries take a bigger share of the trade in goods. But that is only part of the story. I would expect to see a change in the balance of trade in manufactures as well' (Lords Select Committee, Evidence, 15 May 1985, Q.1619). No doubt Dr Pangloss would agree but we beg to differ.

There is no likelihood that the decline of North Sea oil production will make manufacturing workers in British factories work appreciably harder or more effectively. Automatic adjustment will only occur if the run-down in oil production triggers a fall in the real exchange rate and that falling exchange rate then functions as an effective adjustment mechanism. In other words, automaticity depends on the existence of two positive relations: at the national level there has to be a positive relation between oil production and the exchange rate; and at the international level there has to be a positive relation between trade volumes and price relativities. For all the talk of petro-currencies and price competitiveness, it is almost certain that the crucial relations are simply not strong enough to produce smooth automatic adjustment.

We can hardly be confident that the pound will come down because North Sea oil production declines when we are still unsure about whether the pound went up because North Sea oil production was increasing after 1977. Most commentators have argued that high interest rates accounted for the larger part of the appreciation of sterling in this period (Keegan, 1985, pp. 41–2). In its evidence to the Lords Select Committee, the Bank of England claimed that 'of a movement of about 40 per cent in sterling's competitiveness not more than a quarter could reasonably be attributed to North Sea oil' (Lords Select Committee, Evidence, 11 December 1984, Q.215). In the medium term it is now likely that the pound will fall and oil will again play a subsidiary role in that movement; the pound will come under speculative pressure as dealers appreciate that a growing manufacturing trade deficit is creating a fundamental payments disequilibrium. The resulting fall in the value of the pound is unlikely to be a smooth process and it is equally unlikely to damp down manufactured imports and greatly stimulate manufactured exports. Partly this is because 'non-price' factors are the prime determinants of manufacturing trade flows between the advanced industrial countries. It is well known that changes in cost competitiveness do not generally explain changes in national shares of world trade in manufactures (Fetherston, Moore and Rhodes, 1977). Recent British experience suggests that we are no exception to this general rule. As the pound has weakened in the past few years, Britain has had an import boom rather than an export boom. Since 1982, the weighted average of the sterling exchange rate has fallen from 90.7 to 78.8 and the value of manufactured imports has increased by 41.4 per cent while manufactured exports have increased by only 23.7 per cent (*Economic Trends*, September 1985, pp. 50, 77). This is just what one would expect given the reduction of manufacturing capacity and the wholesale liquidation of manufacturing enterprises since 1980. A depreciation of the pound may stimulate exports from the remaining manufacturing firms, but, as the Lords Select Committee Report (p. 42) pointed out, this kind of depreciation will not stimulate a 'sudden re-entry into manufacturing' when production capacity, design skills and distribution networks no longer exist.

Of course, automatic adjustment via the exchange rate is not necessary if the pattern of surpluses and deficits within the payments current account shifts dramatically and the manufacturing deficit diminishes or the service surplus increases. This kind of spontaneous remission is conceivable but it would require a renaissance of British manufacturing and/or a dramatic expansion of the tradeable services sector. We will first examine the possible renaissance of manufacturing because that is the least plausible development. Our argument so far suggests that we cannot expect very much from the existing, or more exactly the surviving, manufacturing firms. Those who expect manufacturing revival expect it to come from new enterprises and new industries. The two most favoured candidates are 'small business' and knowledge-based 'sunrise industries'.

Even if a dynamic small business sector were to develop in Britain, that would not solve our problem about manufacturing trade deficits because small business usually only exports when its components and sub-assemblies are sold abroad inside the finished manufactures of larger companies. Exporting is predominantly the preserve of large enterprises; 80 per cent of our manufacturing exports come from about 100 large companies. As for the new industries, it is equally clear that they will not solve our manufacturing trade deficit problem because our performance in key new industries is as bad or worse than in the old. Consider, for example, the position in information technology (computers, telecommunications and office equipment). In 1978 Britain still had a small favourable trade balance in information technology. By 1983 this became a deficit of £800 million and by 1988 Hewlett Packard estimates the trade deficit will be 'at least £4 billion per annum in electronics alone' (House of Lords Select Committees, 1985, Memorandum by Hewlett Packard). This deficit incidentally arises in the usual way because healthy exports are outweighed by very high levels of import penetration. UK information technology manufactures export a creditable 50 per cent of their production, but the UK market suffers from 58 per cent import penetration. In these terms, the new information technology industry is statistically indistinguishable from the dying industry of car components where export/sales and import penetration ratios are running at very similar levels.

Poor performance in areas like information technology is particularly dispiriting because Britain needs to develop a new knowledge-intensive industrial base. Economic development does depend on major innovations which change the composition of output. New leading sectors (such as motor cars and electrical goods in 1930s Britain or railways in 1840s Britain) are important in redirecting and sustaining economic growth. Furthermore, under intensifying competition from less developed and newly industrialised countries it is clear that the advanced industrial countries are being displaced from old, low-technology, labour-intensive manufacturing lines such as textiles or shoe production. For these reasons, the best prospects for all the advanced industrial countries therefore seem to be in the high value-added, knowledge-based electronics industries of the future. And that really is the problem because, as the information technology deficit figures show, the Japanese, Germans and Americans are currently exploiting the new industrial opportunities more effectively than they did the old. British information technology firms like ICL have been marginalised as minor league producers and are now being subordinated in unequal partnerships with foreign firms like Fujitsu. This result is not surprising when the old manufacturing base has atrophied in Britain; a rapidly declining domestic customer base is a problem that affects ICL as much as ICI. The real importance of the new knowledge-intensive industries is that they interpenetrate and fuse with the old manufacturing base. Having ceded the old industries like cars, the British are now ill-placed to develop the new industries or to transform the old industries with new process technology and modernised products.

If Britain's record in the old or new manufacturing is dire, perhaps we have better prospects in services. It is best to begin here by examining the future of services generally in Britain and in the other advanced economies because this is the context in which services and tradeable services have to be sold. Some still have a vision of a post-industrial future, where we all live by selling services to each other rather than making manufactures. But, realistically, there is little possibility of a general shift from manufacturing into services which would create a new service economy. If we consider the evidence on Britain since 1950, two points stand out. First, the share of expenditure on services in GDP by volume is relatively flat; from 1954 to 1983 that share increased from 47.9 per cent to 50.3 per cent (*Bank of England Quarterly Bulletin*, 1985). Second, the share of expenditure on services in GDP by value rises very slowly; from 1954 to 1983 that share increased from 44.5 to 50.5 per cent (*Bank of England Quarterly Bulletin*, 1985). This evidence is consistent with a consumer income elasticity of demand greater than unity and rising relative prices of services. It is more difficult to increase service productivity so the price of services increases relative to goods and, because consumers want services, in financial terms service expenditure tends to increase slowly. But there is no strong substitution of services for manufactured goods when the volume share of services in GDP is flat. Generally, expansion of services is a kind of money or price illusion.

If we wish to explain these empirical results, we must distinguish between the demand for the final service function and demand for services (Gershuny and Miles, 1983). The demand for the service function in all the advanced economies is high and rising; there is ever-increasing expenditure on, for example, transport and entertainment. But the demand for services does not necessarily rise because in many areas there is competition between services and goods which can discharge a service function; transport or entertainment can be supplied by a privately owned car or VCR rather than by public transport and the cinema. As a result of this widespread competition between goods and services, in the UK economy from 1973 to 1983 the growth rate of expenditure on goods and services was just about equal at 1.3 and 1.4 per cent (*Bank of England Quarterly Bulletin*, 1985). In most areas such as transport, household goods and services, expenditure on goods is increasing materially faster than expenditure on services. Only in 'other services' (mainly financial services) is expenditure on services increasing faster than expenditure on goods. The implication of all this of course is that suppliers of imported manufactures on the British market are doing well out of the increasing demand for the service function; Japanese VCRs, German cars and Italian washing machines are all satisfying demands which would otherwise be met jointly by British producers of sheltered services and manufactures.

Against this background, what reliance can be put on the British suppliers of tradeable services to compensate for the failure of our manufacturers? The trend of the past couple of decades seems to suggest that services could fill any trade gap. In 1963 there was a net deficit on services of £31 million, in 1973 a surplus of £786 million, and in 1983 a surplus of £3,902 million (Lords Select Committee, Department of Trade Memo, 20 November 1984). Preliminary figures for 1984 suggested the upward trend was still continuing and the 1984 surplus would be £4,372 million (*Economic Trends*, March 1985, p. 74). But, at the same time, there are good reasons to be cautious about whether the favourable trend will continue. To begin with, we are large importers of services as well as exporters of services; in the first half of the 1980s our service exports were only 25–30 per cent larger

Table 4.5 Value of service exports as a percentage of the value of service imports by sector

	Sea transport	Civil aviation	Travel	Financial and other services
1976	102.5	124.9	165.5	203.6
1977	102.6	122.2	198.3	206.3
1978	99.6	123.7	161.8	243.0
1979	103.4	119.6	132.6	259.0
1980	103.8	121.7	108.1	264.8
1981	95.9	122.7	90.8	279.0
1982	83.1	118.8	87.0	239.6
1983	75.1	119.1	90.2	243.4
1984	73.7	118.4	90.3	237.3

Source: Economic Trends, September 1985, Table 5, p. 80

than our service imports (*Economic Trends*, September 1985, p. 81). Relatively small shifts in either of the two large totals could wipe out our existing surplus.

Furthermore, our present surplus in services is relatively narrowly based as Table 4.5 shows. Two of the four major sectors are in deficit with sea transport showing a sharp deterioration over the past decade. Civil aviation turns in a modest surplus but it is 'financial and other services' which earn almost all the surplus. These financial and other services account for half of our total service exports. As might be expected from the patchy disaggregated performance, our overall performance in the world market for tradeable services is not at all creditable. From the Bank of England's recent investigation (*Bank of England Quarterly Bulletin*, 1985) it appears that we have been losing our share of world trade in services at least as fast as we have been losing our share of world trade in manufactures.

If our past success in tradeable services is modest, there is not much hope of expanding service exports in the future to fill the widening trade gap caused by manufacturing deficits. To begin with, in the nature of things, tradeable services can only substitute for manufactured exports; they can do little to damp down the growth of manufactured imports which is the heart of our present problem. Furthermore, services account for a much smaller proportion of our exports than do manufactures.

As Table 4.6 shows, in 1984 half of the value of UK exports was made up of manufactures, less than a quarter were accounted for by services, while 'financial and other services' accounted for just 10 per cent. Consequently, as the Lords Select Committee Report (p. 42) notes, a 1 per cent fall in exports of manufactures requires a 3 per cent rise in exports of services to compensate. Underlying all these

Table 4.6   UK exports and imports of goods and services

	Exports			Imports		
	Share of value		Average annual real growth	Share of value		Average annual real growth
	1974	1984		1974	1984	
Fuel	3	17	15.8	15	11	−9.8
Manufactures	56	51	0.9	42	55	6.1
Services of which:						
Sea transport	12	4	−8.7	10	5	−5.6
Air transport	3	3	6.3	2	3	8.1
Tourism	4	5	0.2	3	5	10.0
Financial and other	10	11	2.4	4	5	1.5

Source: Bank of England Quarterly Bulletin, September 1985

problems, there is the fundamental point that many services are naturally sheltered and thus there is a limit on the proportion of service output that can be traded. Many British suppliers of sheltered services are materially damaged by the decline of domestic manufacturing which is caused by stagnant exports and rising imports; the Association of British Chambers of Commerce estimates that 20 per cent of service output is directly sold to manufacturing enterprises (Lords Select Committee Report, p. 42). Given all these considerations, we would be asking too much of the financial service sector if we expect it to plug a widening trade gap caused by manufacturing deficits. It is also true that the immediate export market prospects for our financial service exports are not good; the deregulation of world financial markets inaugurates an era of greater competition in this sector and threatens our established position just as the liberalisation of manufacturing trade did in the 1950s and 1960s foreign trade crises.

No process of automatic adjustment or spontaneous remission will save us from the consequences of poor manufacturing performance which, in a liberal international economic order, is reflected in rising trade deficits. The question is what is to be done and this is the issue which we take up in the remainder of this chapter. We will begin by examining the argument that there is a micro-economic solution (or palliation) for the coming crisis.

(2) Micro solutions

It is always plausible to suppose that the determinants of economic performance are to be found at the level of the enterprise; if the British are bad at manufacturing it may be because the enterprises get it wrong. The handicap of institutional constraints, in the form of the relation to, say, banks and the Stock Exchange, may be admitted. But institutional conditions are not the absolute determinant of manufacturing performance, because there is always scope for manoeuvre at the enterprise level. Thus many would claim that slow innovation, poor product design, inadequate production organisation and inferior marketing are caused by weak and complacent management. On this view, the proper policy solution is to provide an opportunity for enterprises and their managers to get it right. In Britain in the mid-1980s, this general position is developed in two politically differentiated variants. The non-interventionist right puts the main emphasis on the need for a change of managerial culture which will lead to new and more successful business strategies. The centre-left argues a rather different case and emphasises the way in which the state can sponsor a regeneration of manufacturing through an appropriate industrial policy. This section of our chapter will examine both of these positions in turn, beginning with the right-wing argument about the need for a change of management culture. In examining both right and centre-left positions, we will bracket the question of whether the proposed changes are adequate to deal with the impending foreign trade crisis. Instead we will concentrate on the more basic issue of whether a significant improvement in manufacturing performance can be obtained at the micro-economic level by supply-side changes in management culture and/or industrial policy.

The right's micro-economic analysis is politically sponsored. It is developed in endless ministerial speeches which presuppose there is a labour problem; improvements in labour productivity and cost competitiveness are essential; innovation and product-led recovery is the only viable option for our manufacturing enterprises. At the same time, senior government officials dutifully argue that 'there is a limit to the role of government in this area. The main contributions [come] from macro-policies, notably getting down inflation and stimulating competition' (Lords Select Committee, Department of Trade Evidence, 20 December 1984, Q.50). As Chancellor Lawson himself argued, 'the government's job is to create an economic framework' and then let managers get on with the job of managing (Lords Select Committee, Evidence, 15 May 1985, Q.1618). This political analysis is supported by the many industrial managers who have, in Mrs Thatcher's recession, reasserted management's right to manage. The best known managerial supporter of Thatcherite micro-economics is Michael Edwardes who became chairman of British Leyland in 1977 when the company was in crisis. Edwardes's adherence to the right's tenets emerges clearly from his analysis of the car division's problems at that time: 'the company lacked the models, the efficient manufacturing facilities and a management determined to get to grips with over-manning and over-capacity' (Edwardes, 1983, p. 86). His main charge against his predecessors is simply that 'management lost the will to manage' partly because top management failed to back up line management in the divisions. This is the stuff of Thatcherite managerialism.

It is difficult to prove or disprove the right's micro-economic analysis insofar as it consists of so many sweeping generalisations. This suits the government because it provides a kind of irrefutable alibi. No doubt, after she has retired, Mrs Thatcher's memoirs will emphasise that government fulfilled its side of the bargain and created a suitable framework for enterprise culture after 1979; if poor economic performance continues in the late 1980s that must be because managers have not grasped the opportunity that was theirs. But it is possible to examine the right's position critically through case studies whose results are significant even if they are not conclusive. So we propose to examine the success and failure of the Edwardes strategy at BL after 1977, which is a crucial test case for two reasons. First, BL is a major firm in an industry which is at the heart of our manufacturing problems; in 1983, 25 per cent of our manufacturing deficit was in motor vehicles and components and in 1984 this sector accounted for 21 per cent of a larger overall deficit. Second, Edwardes has claimed, and many would argue that 'BL presents a microcosm of the issues affecting British industry as a whole' (Edwardes, 1983, dustjacket; see on cars Williams, K., Williams, J. and Haslam, C., 1986).

In the cars division of BL the negative side of the Edwardes recovery programme was rationalisation, which involved large-scale redundancy and closure of peripheral plants. Capacity in the volume car division was reduced to about 750,000 cars per annum which was not much more than half the notional 1,200,000 capacity of Leyland cars in 1977 (Edwardes, 1983, p. 65). At the same time, the strategy had a positive side because the Edwardes team sought to establish the preconditions for a 'leaner and fitter' cars division which would be moderately profitable and highly productive. There was to be a 'product-led recovery' based on the introduction of a compact model range. Three new models – Metro in 1980, Maestro in 1983 and Montego in 1984 – would sell in volume and push the company's home market share above 20 per cent. While new product lines were being developed, the company invested heavily in automated process technology. The two central manufacturing plants at Longbridge and Cowley were re-tooled at a cost of at least £250 million. Finally, on the industrial relations front, the new management struggled with the problem of 'factories out of control and some virtually controlled by shop stewards' (Edwardes, 1983, p. 292). The struggle with the workforce culminated in management's imposition of new work practices in April 1980. Edwardes left the company in 1983 and by the following year the company had a docile workforce building the full range of new models in automated factories.

The key strategic objectives of increased profit, productivity and market share have not been achieved. To begin with, profits are elusive even though Austin Rover operates in an accounting framework which is designed to minimise losses (Williams and Haslam, 1986a). After achieving a small profit of £3 million in 1983, Austin Rover made a loss of £26 million in 1984. Profits may not be a useful measure of achievement in an industry where several major European car companies are making huge losses; Renault lost £1000 million in 1984. But that is not much consolation when Austin Rover's record on productivity and market share is poor. Austin Rover has made a series of claims about a labour productivity 'miracle' and some academics (e.g. Willman and Winch, 1984) have accepted these claims. The company's claims are about labour productivity at the line and process level where it has invested heavily in automation which is designed to reduce direct labour input. Labour productivity at the divisional level is a more significant measure because that relates total volume car production to the workforce employed in all the Austin Rover factories. The evidence on divisional labour productivity is dispiriting because in 1984, with a workforce of just under 40,000, the company only made eleven cars per man-year. In current European terms this is mediocre. Furthermore, although eleven cars does represent a short-run recovery, it does not represent a miraculous long-run improvement in the company's labour productivity; the old Austin Morris division of the British Leyland Motor Company, managed 8.7 cars per man year in 1972 without benefit of robots (Williams, 1983, p. 255). Austin Rover's record on market share is even more depressing because, as Table 4.7 shows, product-led recovery never happened. In the crisis year of 1980, Austin Rover's market share

Table 4.7 Austin Rover and the UK car market

	Austin Rover sales (000s)	Total market (000s)	Austin Rover share (%)
1975	354	1,194	29.67
1976	340	1,285	26.48
1977	311	1,323	23.51
1978	359	1,591	22.53
1979	327	1,716	19.03
1980	267	1,513	17.66
1981	277	1,484	18.67
1982	268	1,555	17.24
1983	323	1,791	18.01
1984	309	1,749	17.66

Source: Financial Times, 12 January 1985

sank to an all-time low of 17.66 per cent. By spring 1984, the company was selling the full range of new models and yet its market share for 1984 was still 17.66 per cent. By any standard of financial, productive or market achievement, the Edwardes recovery programme failed.

The strategy failed because Edwardes and his team never identified the real problems facing the cars division and wasted effort on irrelevant side issues. To begin with, they did not identify and resolve the company's internal problems, partly because they were irrationally obsessed with the labour problem. The obsession with the labour problem manifested itself most directly in the priority which Edwardes gave to industrial relations reform. After the spring 1980 reform of work practices, management had the absolute and unilateral right to determine manning levels and workpace in all the car factories. Austin Rover also rather theatrically sacked the Longbridge convenor for refusing to accept the 'recovery plan' and insisted on single-figure pay rises which were below the rate of inflation. Throughout the well-publicised confrontation over these issues, management asserted that the labour problem was important and implied that the financial gains from work practice reform and low pay settlements would be considerable. A sober analysis of the economics of the car business suggests rather different conclusions.

When Edwardes took over in 1977 the control of labour costs was an important issue in the cars division. Important labour cost savings were obtained by a policy of mass sacking which belatedly brought the size of the divisional labour force into line with the company's much reduced output. In the boom year of 1972 Austin Morris made 721,000 cars and by the early 1980s Austin Rover was not making much more than half that number of cars. Through the early 1970s Austin Morris employed around 80,000 workers, and it was only after Edwardes arrived in 1977 that the company pushed through the mass sackings which reduced the Austin Rover workforce to under 40,000 by 1983. The crucial point is that, once the policy of mass sacking had normalised labour costs, the economics of the business were such that only small incremental savings could be obtained from reformed work practices and low pay settlements. Bought-in components and materials account for just over half the cost of a finished motor car and, even with the traditional labour-intensive building methods of the early 1970s, direct and indirect hourly labour costs accounted for no more than one-third of the internally controlled costs. Thus, according to the Central Policy Review Staff (1975), the variable (direct and indirect) labour costs accounted for no more than a modest 16 per cent of the total cost of a finished motor car. Reformed work practices and low pay settlements could only save some part of this 'normal' labour cost of 16 per cent.

If part of 16 per cent was doubtless worth having, savings in variable labour costs did not translate into higher profits because the company had problems about abnormally high fixed costs. Low model volume imposes a serious fixed cost penalty because substantial development and tooling costs have to be spread over a small number of units. Consider, for example, the case of the Metro which cost £275 million to develop (Willman, 1984, p. 44). It would be prudent to write off this development charge over a five-year period and on this basis, if the company produces 175,000 Metros per annum (rather than the 350,000 initially planned), each car carries an *extra* development charge of £157. This is a serious handicap in the low-margin small car business. Low model volume is associated with capacity under-utilisation in the new Austin Rover facilities and this latter problem is in itself sufficient to create a crisis about fixed costs. Austin Rover's chairman admits that the company needs a high level of capacity utilisation before it can make a profit; in January 1985 the company needed a volume of around 650,000 cars and capacity utilisation of approximately 80 per cent if it was to earn sufficient profit to cover depreciation and finance new investment (*Financial Times*, 12 January 1985). In the previous year the company had made just 391,000 cars. The economics of the car business are such that survival depends on the management of fixed costs: no car firm can survive the double handicap of low model volume plus capacity utilisation around 50 per cent.

The irony is that throughout the 1980s, Austin Rover's fixed costs have been out of control while the company publicly celebrates its modest achievement in controlling variable costs. This must raise fundamental questions about the competence of the new breed of Thatcherite manager and these doubts are reinforced if we examine the company's approach to automation and new technology which appeared to be a heaven-sent instrument of labour control. Under the old system of 'mutuality' in the 1970s some Longbridge managers had spent up to half their time negotiating pay and conditions. The Metro body shop was the line managers' revenge because here automatic technology could be used to discipline and punish the hitherto recalcitrant workforce. In the new management Utopia the direct workforce would be much smaller and those who remained would have to perform one repetitive operation in a short cycle time so that car body building would bcome like food processing or chemical production where everything flows smoothly at a pace determined by automatic machines. Thus the company laid out the Metro line regardless of capital expense with the simple aim of taking out as much direct labour as possible. On the evidence then available to the company this substitution of capital for labour was economically irrational because internal company documents of the 1970s show that automated body building was not cheaper than traditional methods

(Willman, 1984, pp. 190, 50). These comparisons were made on the assumption of full capacity utilisation in the new highly capital-intensive facilities; at capacity utilisation rates of around 50 per cent in Longbridge, the cost penalties of new technology must be considerable.

Still more culpably, the management team did not realise that the kind of new technology and automation chosen would be crucial to the company's survival prospects. Choice of new production technology was a crucial issue in a company which was a small-scale producer of volume cars after Edwardes's rationalisation. With production volumes of 1.2 to 1.8 million cars per annum, the major European producers made three to five times as many cars per year as Austin Rover. Their best sellers (VW Golf, Ford Escort, Fiat Uno) have individual model volumes of 400,000 plus which roughly equals BL's total output. Recent academic studies (e.g. Altshuler *et al.*, 1984) have suggested that small-scale car producers can survive if they exploit new kinds of smart automation and flexible manufacturing. In principle, this kind of new technology allows the small firm to produce low volume at reasonable cost because manufacturing facilities no longer have to be dedicated to one model and, as in the Fiat Robogate system, several different models can be produced on one line. On the other hand, inflexible automation with dedicated lines will almost certainly exacerbate the fixed cost handicap of small-scale car producers. In this situation the company got it wrong by initially choosing inflexible automation.

The company did exploit flexibility in the early 1980s when it laid out the Maestro/Montego line at Cowley. But it made major mistakes in the late 1970s when it was re-tooling Longbridge to build the Metro. Because Metro sales projections were wildly optimistic, the company built in overcapacity. The Longbridge Metro facility had a theoretical design capacity of 325,000 cars per annum (Willman and Winch, 1984, p. 194), and Austin Rover's chairman has claimed that the company could build 400,000 Metros per annum (Robson, 1982, p. 186). Austin Rover has never built more than 175,000 per annum and in 1984 production sagged to just 145,000 Metros. This would have mattered less if the Longbridge Metro facility had been flexible so that other models could be sent down the lines. But this is impossible because the Longbridge body shop relies on inflexible multi-welders rather than flexible robots; 70 per cent of Metro body welds are done by multi-welder and only 10 per cent by robot (Willman and Winch, 1984, pp. 198, 54). As a direct result, the better part of half the company's production capacity is laid out in an entirely inflexible form. Far from exploiting the potential of flexible manufacturing, in the Metro body shop Austin Rover invested over £100 million in an inflexible manufacturing system that cannot be used to build anything except 200,000 extra Metros which nobody wants to buy.

If we ask why the extra Metros were unsaleable, we are brought to the issue of market limitations. Our analysis has already discovered a major disjuncture between the strategic priorities of management and the real internal problems of the business. More fundamentally, the Edwardes team was mistaken in supposing the key problems were inside the company and therefore Austin Rover's future depended on what it did itself by way of tackling the internal problems of product, process technology and labour productivity. If management had solved the real internal problems, the productive and financial rewards would have been limited because the basic problem was outside the company in the market place where Austin Rover was beset by market limitations. To establish this point, we must analyse the changing nature of competition in the British car market and its implications for Austin Rover.

By the later 1970s the British market was crucial because Austin Rover was effectively pinned down on its home market. In this respect Austin Rover was (and is) different from other European volume car manufacturers like Fiat, Renault or VW who all have substantial export sales; these European producers typically have a larger share of their home market and claim 3–5 per cent of all the other major European markets. Austin Rover's share of the major continental markets is negligible; in France and West Germany it takes just 0.25 per cent of new car sales. This is the result of past neglect and currently difficult market conditions. Profitable export sales are now hard to find with 25 per cent overcapacity in the European car industry and aggressive price competition. Austin Rover's total car exports have averaged just 75–80,000 units in the 1980s and roughly 80 per cent of the cars produced by Austin Rover are sold on the home market. This market was mature and growing very slowly in secular terms but Austin Rover could have lived with a home market whose overall size was limited. The real threat came from changes in the nature of competition on the British market as the indirect competition of the 1960s and 1970s turned into the full-line direct competition of the 1980s.

Back in the 1960s and 1970s, there was little direct competition for home sales because the two major producers (Austin Morris and Ford) sold differentiated products into distinct market segments. Ford served the fleet and business market with its medium-sized rear-wheel drive 'three box' saloons, while Austin Morris sold small front-wheel drive cars to private customers. In this era of indirect competition, Austin Morris did very badly because its market segment was shrinking and increasingly fiercely contested by importers who sold to private buyers; with the rise of the company car, by the mid-1970s private buyers accounted for just 60 per cent of the market and half these private buyers were choosing imports (Williams *et al.*, 1983, p. 235). Ten years later, Austin Rover is still trapped in the private customer segment because, even after the launch of the Montego in 1984, Austin Rover's share of the company car market is stuck around 15 per cent. If the company has not solved its old market problems, it now faces new and more threatening problems.

The most obvious recent change in the British car market has been the emergence of a third major producer. Vauxhall has come back from the dead and threatens to take 20 per cent of home market sales with the aid of General Motors' financial and design resources. The 'majors' still sell around 65 per cent of the market but that volume is now split three ways between Austin Rover, Ford and Vauxhall. The resurrection of Vauxhall is significant because it intensifies a new pattern of full-line direct competition in the three market classes (small, light and medium) which together account for 85 per cent of new car sales in Britain. In each class, the majors now have three similarly packaged models which have been carefully product-planned to win sales by attracting every available private and business customer. Table 4.8 shows the line-up of directly competing models.

Table 4.8   Full line direct competition with Austin Rover models

Small class	Ford Fiesta
	Austin Metro
	Vauxhall Nova
Light class	Ford Escort/Orion
	Austin Maestro
	Vauxhall Astra
Medium class	Austin Montego
	Ford Sierra
	Vauxhall Cavalier

This kind of full-line direct competition is a very recent development. It began in 1977 when Ford entered the small car class with the Fiesta, and the development was completed in 1983–4 when Vauxhall entered the small car class with the Nova and Austin re-entered the medium class with the Montego.

Full-line direct competition has major implications for Austin Rover. To begin with, the new pattern of competition reduces the volume which can be obtained on the British market with one model in any market class. It becomes increasingly difficult for any major to produce a class-dominating best seller which claims 10 per cent plus of the market as the old Cortina and Escort did. Table 4.9 on the top ten best sellers of 1984 shows how sales in each class are being increasingly split between two or more best sellers from different majors. The

Table 4.9 The top ten best selling cars in Britain, 1984

Ford Escort	9.0 per cent
Vauxhall Cavalier	7.6
Ford Fiesta	7.2
Austin Metro	6.7
Ford Sierra	6.5
Austin Maestro	4.7
Vauxhall Astra	3.2
Vauxhall Nova	3.2
Ford Orion	2.9
Volvo 300	2.0

Source: Society of Motor Manufacturers and Traders, 1984

Escort/Orion retains the old 10 per cent magic. But in the small and medium classes, sales are fairly evenly divided between Fiesta and Metro or Sierra and Cavalier. The top ten account for just over 50 per cent of all car sales and volume sales are fairly evenly divided between the three market classes. So an average best seller from one of the majors now takes just 5 per cent of the market.

This development has repercussions for Austin Rover's overall market share. With a compact model range, the company's overall share will be the sum of the market shares taken by its three volume sellers. It is becoming increasingly difficult to take 20 per cent of the market with two or three models as Austin-Morris did in the 1960s and Ford did in the 1970s.

As Table 4.10 shows, thanks to the Escort, Ford can still pull off

Table 4.10 Share of the British car market claimed by Austin Rover, Ford and Vauxhall's three best selling models

	1975	*1976*	*1977*	*1978*	*1979*	*1980*	*1981*	*1982*	*1983*	*1984*
Austin	19.0	16.1	13.8	13.3	11.9	10.5	12.2	11.7	13.4	13.4
Ford	19.9	22.4	20.1	20.3	22.4	26.8	27.8	26.5	25.3	22.7
Vauxhall	7.3	8.3	8.4	7.8	6.0	6.0*	5.0*	10.9	12.0	13.9

*Two models only

Source: Society of Motor Manufacturers and Traders, 1984

the three-car trick. But arithmetic is working against Austin Rover and Vauxhall. Three models selling an average 5 per cent of the market will claim 15 per cent and, as Table 4.9 shows, this was just about what Austin Rover and Vauxhall did achieve.

The conclusion must be that external problems of market limitation were crucial and full-line direct competition was a sufficient condition for the failure of the Edwardes strategy. The objective of increasing market share to over 20 per cent with just three models was always unrealistic because three times 5 per cent equals a market share of 15 per cent, not 21 or 22 per cent. Again this raises questions about the relevance and competence of Thatcherite management because the Edwardes team never revised sales projections for the Metro, projections which dated from the early 1970s (Willman and Winch, 1984, p. viii) and which were wildly optimistic after 1977 when Ford had entered the small car class with the Fiesta; Austin Rover projected sales of 350,000 Metros per annum but thanks to the Fiesta has predictably never sold more than half that number.

It should also be emphasised that the continued operation of market limitations compromised the company's position and ensures that it must now retreat from manufacturing Austins into assembling Hondas. In a fragmenting market, when the new Edwardes models would not sell in high volume, the deletion of old low-volume models reduced the company's market share. In the event, 80 per cent of the decline in Austin Rover's UK registrations between 1973 and 1983 was accounted for by the deletion of a variety of old models, like the Maxi and the Dolomite, which regularly figured between positions 4 and 10 in the UK best sellers' chart. If Austin Rover wanted to improve market share, the company needed a broad range of models which in a fragmented market would always sell at low volume. The only profitable way of obtaining such models is by assembling Hondas like the Ballade which has been sold as the Triumph Acclaim/Rover 213 in a volume of around 50,000 per annum. The implication of all this is that, if Austin Rover's manufacturing capability is to be preserved, it is necessary to take some form of political action which safeguards Austin Rover's home market by changing the composition of demand. When a sober analysis of market difficulties leads to this explosive conclusion, it is perhaps not surprising that Edwardes, as the government-appointed chairman of a major nationalised enterprise, chose to concentrate on other safer issues such as the labour problem.

As academics, we are not inhibited in the same way, and we believe it is important to emphasise the market causes of failure especially because Austin Rover's problems are typical of those which arise in the other problem sectors of British manufacturing. Overall, British manufacturing exports a healthy proportion of output which rose steadily towards 32 per cent over the decade of the 1970s (Williams *et al.*, 1983, p. 119). But in problem sectors, like consumer electronics or white goods as well as cars, during the long boom enterprises failed to build up export and/or have since lost exports to traditional markets. British enterprises can be then wiped out just like Austin Rover. In a situation of market fragmentation the British enterprise's traditionally large share of the home market is inevitably eroded by importers who take scale away from the British producer who is increasingly marginalised as a high-cost, small-volume producer.

Mainland European producers survive similar processes of fragmentation on their home markets with the aid of export sales to near European markets. The Japanese prosper from fragmentation in all the European markets because they export and assemble everywhere with the aid of a government which reserves their domestic market for Japanese manufacturers. When the dynamics of market retreat and enterprise collapse are similar, the history of Austin Rover in cars is the history of Ferguson and GEC in consumer electronics or Hotpoint and Hoover in white goods. The brand names are different and the parent enterprises are at different stages of retreat but the paradigm of market-led failure is always the same.

In their rather different way the centre-left, just like the right, prefers to dream of product-led recovery rather than face the reality of market-led failure. The difference is that the centre-left accepts that the problems of an uncompetitive manufacturing sector cannot be entirely solved at the enterprise level and that piecemeal microeconomic intervention by the state is necessary. On this view, the imperfect signals of the market need supplementing if industrial regeneration is to be achieved; the state can and must supply overall co-ordination of sectoral activity, allow managers to take a long view of investment and generally support product and process innovation. An active industrial policy can thus refresh the parts that the free market does not. As the failure of the right's approach becomes more obvious, so industrial policy attracts increasing support from centre-left political parties; the current British Labour Party 'jobs and industry' campaign is evidence of this. But it remains true that the case for industrial policy has been most powerfully argued by academics and intellectuals. This point emerges clearly if we examine centrist analyses of the current crisis in Britain and in America which has similar but less acute problems about an uncompetitive manufacturing sector. Two pertinent analyses are provided by Smith's (1984) *British Economic Crisis* and Magaziner and Reich's (1982) *Minding America's Business*.

Smith puts considerable emphasis on deficiencies in British research and development; the level of such expenditure has been inadequate and British expenditure has been misdirected because too much has been allocated to military and prestige projects like nuclear power and civil aircraft. Manufacturing competitiveness has inevitably suffered because 'the projects in which [manufacturing] investment has been embodied have not had the degree of research and development input which generates the design and production quality on which real market success is based' (Smith, 1984, p. 204). Magaziner and Reich are more generally concerned with the design of a new kind of industrial policy which has the double aim of easing the social costs of business decline where that is inevitable and of obtaining competitive advantage in growing businesses where that is possible. In the latter case the government can solve particular industrial problems by selective policies which involve funding research and development where public and private returns diverge, subsidising high-risk investments, supporting key linkage industries which are strategic for others, sharing the costs of developing foreign markets and subsidising the cost of education and training. This kind of targeted industrial policy supervised by one small central government department (like MITI in Japan) is very different from the non-discriminatory and general industrial policies of the traditional British type; Magaziner and Reich reject general investment allowances or tax rebates on exports as expensive and ineffective policy instruments.

Smith's analysis and prescriptions are necessarily limited because he works within the framework of orthodox economic theory. From this point of view, the problem is one of inputs to, and outputs from, the production process. Poor manufacturing performance must thus be the result of the failure of some input into the growth and structural transformation process. The old centre-left economists' 1960s excuse for poor British manufacturing performance was too little investment; Smith accepts that this is implausible because since 1945 the British have maintained levels of investment in machinery and equipment which compare respectably with those of our competitors despite the disincentive of a low British rate of return. Smith's new centre-left economists' 1980s explanation for poor British manufacturing performance is not enough intelligent investment; in this context it is significant that Smith defines research and development as 'the process by which opportunities for profitable investment are found' (Smith, 1984, p. 198). More fundamental problems about differences in the organisation of production in various national economies largely escape Smith because of his commitment to the theoretical framework of orthodox economics which aspires to provide a theory of the capitalist economy in general (Cutler *et al.*, 1978, vol. 2). As we have argued elsewhere (Williams *et al.*, 1983), the resulting theory necessarily abstracts from differences in specifically national institutional conditions and from the discretionary and variable nature of enterprise calculation.

Magaziner and Reich come from a rather different intellectual background in management consultancy and American business schools. The great virtue of their analysis of the American situation is that they do see that differences in variable institutional structures and discretionary enterprise calculation are important because variability in these external conditions and internal forms of calculation is probably the major cause of divergencies in manufacturing performance amongst the advanced countries. Thus, for example, Magaziner and Reich argue that government industrial policy is not enough if American enterprises continue to use mechanical Return on Investment (ROI) techniques and use financial ratios to guide their major investment decisions. Instead they recommend that American enterprises identify and exploit the sources of competitive cost leverage which include purchasing, manufacturing, marketing and distribution, application, engineering and research and development. These sources of advantage are specific to particular businesses and thus there are no general rules for investment decisions. All this amounts to a progressive problem shift away from economics although, as we have argued elsewhere (Williams, 1984; Williams and Haslam 1986(b)), Magaziner and Reich's positions should not be accepted uncritically.

On the crucial issue of targeted industrial policy, Magaziner and Reich are particularly unconvincing. They do not answer the overwhelming question about according to what criteria, or after what process of calculation, does a government agency pick winners and identify losers. This question can hardly be avoided when the record of American (or British) government agencies in the industrial policy field is discouraging. Magaziner and Reich's arguments about doctoring losers and picking winners are riddled with absences and omissions. They provide no clear guide to identifying losers and do not explain what should be done for traditional basic industries, like steel or motor cars, which are in serious trouble all over Europe and North America. For example, are these industries declining industries whose migration to Japan or Korea should be hastened; or are they key 'linkage industries' which should be maintained because of their backward and forward linkages to the rest of the economy? Equally disconcertingly, Magaziner and Reich are no more explicit about picking winners. They provide a list of high-tech businesses of the future (high technology, fibre optics, lasers, computers, etc.). But that list is not an operational guide to sponsoring particular enterprises and projects in specific areas and such a guide would seem to be necessary if, as Magaziner and Reich argue, there are no simple general rules for investment appraisal. Even judgment by the observed results of government policy is not easy because industrial policy is to some extent a self-fulfilling prophecy when, according to Magaziner and Reich, losers should be denied the resources to become competitive and winners should be given the necessary resources. In such cases we would never know whether government made the right policy decisions. When Magaziner and Reich cannot answer the overwhelming question about criteria, industrial policy inevitably becomes a mystery.

Although they cannot explain how it works, the advocates of industrial policy have no doubt that it does. Both Smith and Magaziner and Reich try to establish this point in the now conventional way by pointing to the example of Japan where industrial policy promotes manufacturing success. If this success can hardly be disputed, the question is to what extent it can be attributed to industrial policy. Does Japan show that industrial policy is a powerful instrument which can transform manufacturing uncompetitiveness into competitiveness? Or do the advocates of industrial policy rest their case on a misreading of Japanese experience?

To begin with, we must deal with the argument that Japanese success rests on unique cultural institutions. The extent and significance of some of these differences has been greatly exaggerated. Consider, for example, the case of Japanese labour institutions and, more specifically, the practice of 'lifetime' or permanent employment. In Japan this practice is limited to *male* employees in large firms (Cole, 1972, p. 615) and lifetime employment is by no means universal within such firms (Kendal, 1984, p. 73). Consequently, the pattern of security of employment in Japan is not so very different from that which prevails in other advanced countries. Hall's (1982) study in the United States shows that about 50 per cent of men aged over 35 can expect eventually to work twenty years for one employer and 40 per cent of men aged over 55 had worked more than twenty years for one employer. It is also true that the economic significance of lifetime employment has been exaggerated. Formal guarantees of permanent employment in Japan may produce a more committed and flexible workforce. But this can only be a source of competitive advantage if management has a positive strategy for organising production; as the Austin Rover case shows, with a deficient management strategy all the worker 'flexibility' and commitment in the world is inconsequential.

In a capitalist manufacturing system, labour can play a secondary role by frustrating management initiatives but the quality of the results will be primarily determined by managerial initiative. If the results are better in Japan, that is likely to be because their managers' organisation of production and marketing is superior. In the area of production, the Japanese have certainly established a new standard of excellence. They have learnt how to combine the advantages of scale and scope. In all their areas of success, the Japanese have achieved scale advantages. They have the largest steel works, the world's best-selling car and the highest cumulative volume in most kinds of consumer electronics: in TV sets, for example, at the end of the 1970s, the average Japanese factory produced 700,000 sets per annum compared with 150,000 per annum in the UK, and cumulative volume for each chassis type in Japan averaged 1.2 million which is three times the European norm (Magaziner and Hout, 1980). The Japanese trick is to exploit scale without suffering the inflexibility disadvantages associated with the earlier US style automation which produced long runs of a standard product. Furthermore, Japanese labour and capital productivity is not completely dependent on the radical re-design of product and process technology although, of course, those sources of advantage are also aggressively pursued. Substantial improvement in quality and productivity can be achieved without recourse to over specialised capital equipment. Using a given process technology, the Japanese will take labour time out and improve capital utilisation through fine-tuning and attention to detail; the inexpensive modification of punch presses at Kawasaki, Lincoln to allow quicker die changes is a classic example of this attention to detail (Schonberger, 1982).

Ultimately Japanese productive success does not depend on superior machinery; it would indeed be difficult to sustain any advantage on this basis because, in industries like cars, similar equipment is used in car factories throughout the world. The Japanese advantage rests on superior techniques for organising production. Toyota, for example, has developed a 'just in time' production system based on Kanban cards. A withdrawal Kanban allows an upstream production station (b) to claim no more parts than are immediately required to keep station (b) operating, and a production Kanban prevents the downstream production station (a) from producing more parts than are withdrawn for use. By this means, excess production stocks are eliminated at every stage in the production process, and the same system is applied to outside component suppliers who are expected to make several small deliveries on each working day. The Kanban technique is basically a simple one but its benefits are considerable. The direct benefit is a reduction in expensive inventories, but significant indirect benefits are also obtained. Product quality has to be raised because, with minimal inventories, defective parts hold up production. Productivity also increases for a variety of reasons: with minimum inventories, bottlenecks on the production line are exposed and have to be removed if production is to proceed smoothly; and with small-lot production, machine set-up time has to be reduced if unproductive down time is to be controlled. The kinds of just-in-time production techniques pioneered by Toyota increasingly blur the distinction between repetitive manufacturing and automated process technology.

Superior Japanese manufacturing techniques have a dramatic impact on production costs and quality. The Japanese smoothly take labour time out of the product while their competitors stagnate or take labour time out at a much slower rate; in cars, for example, the Japanese reduced the number of build hours per car from 250 to 140 hours during the 1970s while the West Germans could not manage any reduction at all (Altshuler *et al.*, 1984, p. 160). Savings in labour costs are not in themselves crucial but combined with economy in the use of capital equipment and unique scale-plus-scope advantages, the result is ever-lower production costs. Recent estimates suggest that the Japanese can produce a small car for \$1200–1500 less than the Americans and \$500–700 less than the Europeans (Abernathy, Clark and Kantrow, 1981, p. 73; Altshuler *et al.*, 1984, pp. 155, 158). As every consumer knows, the Japanese manufacturing system also produces a more reliable product; consumer magazines around the world confirm the superior reliability of Japanese cars and consumer electronics. In some product areas, the differences in reliability in use are staggering; Garvin's (1983) recent study of American and Japanese manufactured air conditioning units showed that the US median for service calls in the first year was over seventeen times the Japanese rate and the best US producer made two and a half times as many service calls per 100 units as the worst Japanese producer.

The Japanese manufacturing system depends on the back-up of an appropriate marketing system. The manufacturing system works through the production of increasing volumes of existing product lines and higher value-added is obtained through the ceaseless development of existing products and the introduction of new ones. The Japanese then use highly stereotyped marketing techniques to shift increasing volumes of product. We can analyse and illustrate these marketing tactics by examining the classic case of Japanese motor bikes (Boston Consulting Group, 1975). Similar tactics have since been used in cars, consumer electronics, photocopiers and construction equipment.

- Production volume is initially built up on the protected home market. The big three Japanese motor bike producers began as mass producers of step-through commuter bikes for Japanese workers.
- Export market opportunities are carefully identified. The Japanese had the marketing *savoir faire* to appreciate that their mass production skills could be applied to producing reliable, low-cost larger-capacity bikes for the American secondary use (leisure) market which had traditionally been supplied by British craft producers.
- The Japanese take a long-run view of an export market's potential. In motor bikes the Japanese were prepared to undertake expensive investment in distribution and parts back-up. They also set sales targets in terms of market share rather than short-term profit.
- As new entrants, the Japanese use 'laser beam' targeting and predatory pricing to gain entrance into a few peripheral markets or market segments. In motor bikes, the Japanese began by producing small capacity bikes and then moved up the market class by class so that the European and American craft producers retreated into making superbikes with capacities of more than 750cc.
- When the Japanese are a major force in the market, product differentiation is used as a marketing tool. Thus the Japanese developed trail and farm bikes so as to exploit new higher value-added segments of demand and occupy every niche in the market.

- When weaker European and American competitors have been eliminated in sales wars, and when the perceived quality of the Japanese product is established, it will be sold at a premium price. Cheap and nasty motor bikes come from non-Japanese factories.
- The ultimate marketing problem is saturation of the world market for one product. In motor bikes this point was reached at the end of the 1970s. In the long run, the marketing system therefore requires a constant procession of new products; compact disc players, VCRs and 'Walkman' personal stereos must be developed to sell alongside mature products like colour TVs and conventional cassette players.

If the dynamics of the production and marketing system are relatively clear, the role of government industrial policy in Japan is much more confused. Government policy is important in some respects because it has at least established some preconditions for the development of the manufacturing and marketing system. Protection of the home market is the most important of these preconditions; industries like cars and consumer electronics were all protected in their infancy. Effective restriction of foreign access to the home market remains important. We think of Japan as the 'super exporter' but home demand is more important to Japanese manufacturers than it is in other advanced countries; as Table 4.11 shows, Japanese exports account for a smaller proportion of GDP than in any major European country.

Table 4.11 Exports (free on board) as a percentage of gross domestic product

1982	
France	17.13%
Germany	26.60%
Italy	21.28%
Japan	13.02%
UK	20.63%
USA	7.02%

Source: OECD, 1984

But if we examine any of the standard accounts of the 'brilliant success' of MITI's industrial policy (e.g. Magaziner and Hout, 1980), we find some disturbing anomalies. When it comes to picking winners, Japanese policy makers are not always successful. In the period of emergence in the 1950s, Japanese civil servants backed valves rather than transistors and promoted the one people's car concept (Magaziner and Hout, 1980). In this period, when Japan was a 'follower country', there was effectively a plan which targeted businesses like

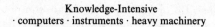

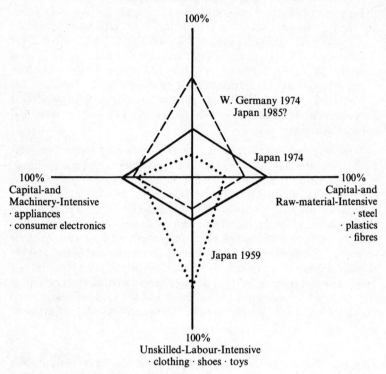

Source: Japanese Economic Planning Agency, reproduced in Magaziner and
       Reich, 1982, p. 80
Figure 4.4 Evolution of industrial structure

steel and cars where national producers were initially only required
to master the available Western techniques of production. But in
recent years, there does not seem to have been any plan except for
the much reproduced diamond-shaped diagram of industrial development which establishes the desirability of high-value-added, knowledge-intensive industries. This provides no guide to choosing particular projects in high technology areas. It is also notable that, in
terms of authority, Japanese policy makers do not have absolute
power. The state failed to obtain consolidation of ownership in cars
and car components in the 1960s or in computers in the 1970s (Magaziner and Hout, 1980). In some ways the Japanese conglomerate
structure is peculiarly well adapted to resisting government because

many major manufacturing firms have their own 'in house' sources of finance. In practice, government/industry conflicts and differences of opinion, like that created by the unauthorised expansion of Sumitomo Steel, seem to have been eased by headlong national expansion.

In weighting the relative significance of Japanese industrial policy against manufacturing and marketing techniques, it is important to avoid factorialism. Clearly, it would be wrong to abstract one item from a complex combination where it is the relation between the items which guarantees the end result. From this point of view, however, the primary force in the combination is the unique productive and market system whose immanent tendency is ever-higher volume and value-added achieved through the sale of new and existing products in whatever markets are available. Protection of the home market is important but other more interventionist kinds of industrial policy appear to play a very secondary role. To make the same point another way, one might say that in Japan the production and marketing system is such that the industrial policy makers' task is easy; the logic of the manufacturing-cum-marketing system is so powerful that it is not difficult to pick winners and it hardly matters if the government backs the occasional loser. If these conclusions are accepted, it is difficult to see how industrial policy is a powerful instrument which the British (or Americans) could use to transform manufacturing competitiveness; if it is grafted on to a second-rate productive and marketing system industrial policy may well have very little efficacy at all. The micro-economic lesson of the Japanese experience is not that Britain could choose the right industrial policy but that Britain is lumbered with the wrong manufacturing and marketing system.

That is a pretty dispiriting conclusion because, as we shall now argue, it is not easy to imitate the superior Japanese productive and marketing techniques. To begin with, the Japanese marketing machine makes it very difficult for other producers to survive. The Japanese seek to capture volume sales and do so by fulfilling the whole range of a distributor's needs and occupying every niche in the final product market. Thus in cars at present the Japanese are proliferating 'tall cars', people carriers, performance and utility four-wheel drives, sporting cars and luxury cars. European car producers who occupy, or retreat into, specialist niches will shortly feel as threatened as the mass producers. As the Japanese producers move up-market, they do leave some niches in the production of low-value-added low-technology items. But these are usually occupied by the low-wage newly industrialised countries; thus in consumer electronics, the Japanese firms merchandise and organise the production of cheap radio cassettes in Taiwan and Singapore. There are not many pickings here for the advanced industrial countries. Much discussion of Japanese marketing techniques is concerned with the predatory new entrant tactics of Japanese enterprises and many commentators (e.g. Magaziner and Reich, 1982) recommend Western firms to imitate these tactics. This is naive because the capability of the Japanese production system underwrites and justifies the predatory marketing tactics; the Japanese factories can always deliver a low-cost, higher-quality, market-leading product in the long run if entrance can be negotiated and a market presence can be established in the short run. Western firms like IBM or GM are willing and able to use predatory marketing tactics; this is just what GM is doing with Vauxhall cars in Britain where it is buying market share. But, without the back-up of Japanese production excellence, these tactics will not automatically produce beneficial results; the predatory Western major is usually dissipating financial resources for short-run gains and the longer-term outcome is entirely uncertain.

If copying Japanese marketing tactics is to be worthwhile, Western enterprises must first copy the Japanese production systems, and that is very difficult. In this respect the new techniques are radically different from the original Fordist techniques of mass production which were easily imitated by any enterprise which could find scale. Japanese management overseas can reproduce the magic formula. They obtain dramatic quality improvements even where they take over an existing plant. Juran (1978) cites the case of a TV plant which had been owned by the US firm Motorola; under the new Japanese management, the defect rate per 100 sets fell from 150–180 to just 3–4. But such performance improvements have a limited effect because the Japanese, for obvious reasons, prefer to build satellite assembly plants in Europe and America. It is difficult for independent Western managements to make the required improvement in performance because Japanese manufacturing techniques are a complex whole; simply introducing 'quality circles' will not revolutionise production techniques. There is also the problem that Japanese firms are constantly improving their performance so that Western firms have to hit a moving target. In 1973 Japanese electronics firms took 3.4 man hours to assemble a standard TV set and American firms took 4.8 hours; by 1979 the Americans had very creditably reduced the assembly requirement to 2.6 man hours per set and the Japanese had reduced the assembly requirement to just 0.8 man hours per set (Magaziner and Reich, 1982, p. 113). After heroic efforts and considerable improvement, the American TV producers ended up even further behind.

In this context, British management can hardly be relied upon to close any productive efficiency gap because their mediocrity is almost a natural polar opposite to Japanese excellence. The disorganisation of production in British enterprises has often been blamed on obstructive unions. This excuse can hardly be plausibly used any more when the unions have been tamed by recession and mass unemployment. The most recent study (Daly, Hitchens and Wagner, 1985) shows that the disorganisation is as bad as ever. The basic British mistake is to suppose that manufacturing efficiency can be obtained by buying in modern machines; all the recent surveys show that the stock of machinery in British factories is as, or more, up-to-date as in German or US factories (see Daly *et al.*, 1985). Given unlimited funds, British management often pursues hypothetical economies of scale by investment in new, larger-scale capital equipment; as we have argued elsewhere (Williams and Haslam, 1986b), this was what did happen in the 1970s in nationalised coal, steel and cars. But in manufacturing it is not what you have but how you use it that really counts. Daly *et al*'s (1985) pilot study shows that metalworking machinery in British factories is used less effectively than in German factories. It is generally set up less well because numerical control devices and automatic feeders have not been fitted. It is also worse maintained and frequent break-downs are a problem particularly with more sophisticated equipment. Where machines are sophisticated, British management often does not understand what the machines can do. There is no easy cure for this pervasive lack of technical expertise in the micro level.

Japanese techniques allow for substantially greater efficiency in the production of manufactured goods and to that extent we must imitate them. On the other hand we should not suppose that imitation will allow us to survive against them in a context of free competition. It is interesting to note that most Western governments have already drawn this conclusion. Motor vehicles account for nearly 30 per cent of Japanese exports to the US and nearly 20 per cent of Japanese exports to Europe. And almost everywhere domestic car producers are protected from Japanese competition. Since 1975 the UK has had an unofficial agreement with Japan to limit car imports to 11 per cent of the UK market, since 1976 Italy has operated a ceiling of only 2,200 Japanese car imports per annum and since 1977 France has imposed a 3 per cent market share ceiling on Japanese imports (Altshuler *et al.*, 1984, pp. 231–2). The US has only recently lifted import restrictions on Japanese cars and no other advanced country is likely to follow this lead. With the current exception of the USA, no major car-producing country is practising 'free trade' with Japan. For Britain, which suffers from peculiarly severe problems of pro-ductive disorganisation, the question must be whether and how we should extend protection to other product lines. This question is taken up in the next section.

(3) **Macro solutions and constraints**

In classic liberal collectivism, piecemeal intervention did not play a large role. The liberal collectivists hoped that some form of indirect macro-economic intervention, through socialisation of investment or demand management, would be enough to maintain full employment and incidentally solve most of our other problems. For the wilder kinds of monetarists or rational expectations theorists, even this is too interventionist. But the notion that the state can renounce macro policy as the work of the (collectivist) devil is naive; *de facto*, as long as the state spends a sizeable slice of the national income, there has to be some kind of macro-economic 'policy' or at least a fiscal stance which has definite effects on the level and composition of output. Therefore it is reasonable to ask whether we can use macro policies constructively to solve the problems about foreign trade which were outlined in the first section of this chapter. We will open the argument by establishing the point that, if orthodox macro policies operate in a liberal collectivist framework, they cannot solve our problem. We then go on to argue that, if we break with this framework, protectionist policies can offer some relief.

In the space available, we cannot review the whole range of macro-economic policy instruments or the debates between monetarists and Keynesians about the efficacy of the various instruments. Instead, we propose to concentrate on the prospects and possibilities for Keynesian reflation which could stimulate domestic consumption and/or promote infrastructural investment. It is appropriate to concentrate on such strategies because they are lineally descended from what Keynes proposed in the *General Theory*. The fiscal expansion of demand is of course very different from the socialisation of investment which Keynes proposed in 1936. But the 1940 pamphlet *How to Pay for the War* represents Keynes's own later conversion to demand management. And, as Beveridge's *Full Employment* (1944) shows, the techniques which were applied to damping down excess demand during the Second World War could easily be applied to stimulating demand in the post-war world. Apart from its intellectual pertinence, reflation is politically relevant because, since the emergence of mass unemployment in the 1970s, reflation in one form or another has been the left and centre-left's favoured macro panacea for our most obvious problems; from this point of view, it is supposed that a centre or left government should be less wary of inflation and could stimulate demand to absorb some of our unemployment. As the centrist Charter for Jobs groups argues, 'the first thing is to adopt less deflationary budgetary policies, in order to reduce the demand deficient component of our unemployment' (Charter for Jobs, 1985, p. 15).

Such proposals raise a variety of issues. Not least, they raise the question of to what extent, in an earlier era, Keynesian demand management policies guaranteed prosperity in the long boom of the 1950s and 1960s. As we have discussed these issues elsewhere (Williams *et al.*, 1983, pp. 96–9), we propose to concentrate on the immediate issue of whether Keynesian reflation will work for Britain now in the context of recession and slump. We will do this by analysing the French experience in 1982–3, which provides us with a crucial test of Keynesianism's efficacy in this context. The reflation introduced by the Mitterand government was a modest one; the package only raised production to a level which was 1 per cent higher than it would otherwise have been. It failed when it only delayed further increases in unemployment. As Glyn (1985) argues, there were two causes of failure. First, public and private investment was not planned and a linked co-ordinated expansion of major industrial sectors was not obtained. The French government's nationalisation programme had provided it with considerable leverage in this area because more than half of industrial investment was in the newly nationalised groups, but the Mitterand government never used this lever. Second, even though French manufacturing is somewhat more competitive than British and the French did not have a manufacturing trade deficit, the French encountered a foreign trade constraint. The French government would not contemplate import controls and, as the economy was stimulated, imports rose, the balance of payments deteriorated and the franc came under pressure. Mitterand's administration responded in the orthodox way with devaluation and deflationary cuts which by 1983 had offset all the initial expansionary impetus.

If socialism in one country was problematic in the 1930s, the French experience shows that Keynesianism in one medium-sized country is impossible in the 1980s. In just the same way, the experience of the Labour government in 1974 shows that in a deflationary world, balance of payments deficits and currency crises block the road of national reflation. If it is impossible to break out of recession by unilateral action, some would argue that this establishes the case for a co-ordinated European reflation. This possibility is often raised very diffidently; in *Britain Without Oil*, Keegan (1985, p. 105), claims only that 'one has to start, or start again somewhere'.

There are good reasons for being diffident about the prospects of co-ordinated reflation. To begin with, such policies require an international political consensus which cannot be easily achieved; there is little prospect of agreement on common reflationary policies when the French, German, Italian and British governments are separated by differences of political ideology and national circumstance. Furthermore, as Keegan honestly recognises, 'how the British would fare in a co-ordinated expansion remains to be seen' (Keegan, 1985, p. 105). In fact, it is fairly certain that the British would do badly and our foreign trade constraint would not be eased. Substantial differences in national manufacturing capability have persisted for more than thirty years and they would only reassert themselves in slightly different form in the new Keynesian world of co-ordinated reflation. This is inevitable when reflation (co-ordinated or otherwise) does not sort out micro-economic problems; such macro policies will not create a BL dealer network in Germany or solve the disorganisation of production in BL factories.

Reflation could be backed with various correlative policies. But the policies which are usually advocated for this purpose will not make Keynesianism more effective in dealing with unemployment or ease the trade constraint. Centrist politicians and academics often advocate incomes policy as an instrument which can obtain a better trade-off between inflation and unemployment where reflation is being attempted. But, as the economic literature on British incomes policies in the 1960s and 1970s shows, incomes policy does not work for long; the dam bursts and there is a catching-up phase after the initial freeze has expired. This is more or less inevitable under the British system of two-tier collective bargaining where plant level settlements cannot be policed. Furthermore, incomes policy is irrelevant at the micro level where our difficulties arise. At the enterprise or industry level, Britain's manufacturing's problem is *non-price* competitiveness; and, as we have argued elsewhere (Williams *et al.*, 1983, pp. 34–47) the level of labour costs is not a crucial source of advantage or disadvantage in industries and enterprises whose cost problems are often caused by other problems such as small scale. The more radical left would argue for correlative policies of institutional reform, especially reform of financial institutions. The British Labour party currently proposes the creation of a National Investment Bank and the Lords Select Committee more cautiously recommended that investment funds be made more cheaply available. Such policies are, like incomes policies, worthwhile but they would have a limited short-run impact. Financially, they would create new and more favourable permissive conditions but manufacturing enterprises would still be free to make their own conservative financial calculations as GEC did through the 1970s (Williams *et al.*, 1983, pp. 132–78). Furthermore any favourable effects would be very gradual; a National Investment Bank would not have much impact on this year's dole queue or next year's manufacturing trade deficit.

The conclusion must be that, in orthodox liberal collectivist terms, we are boxed in at the macro level. With or without the conventional correlative policies, a national or international programme of Keynesian reflation would draw in imports to Britain and simply hasten the pending foreign trade crisis and its deflationary final solution. Keynesian reflation is immediately not enough to solve our problems and ultimately, after the deflationary solution has been imposed, it may be counter-productive in its effects on output and employment. Our analysis of the French experience shows us the reason why the effects are so disappointing. The problem of orthodox macro policy is that liberal collectivists will the end but cannot contemplate the necessary means. Domestically, they accept the undesirability of state control over the decision making of capitalist manufacturing enterprises. Internationally, they accept the desirability of free trade. If macro-economic policy is to work usefully for us, we must break with liberal collectivism at both these crucial points and move the whole debate about policy on to the terrain which is forbidden by liberal collectivism.

Immediately, in the next section of this chapter, we wish to take up the issue of justifying the break with free trade. This is because it is politically and intellectually easier to make the arguments against free trade rather than the arguments for socialist planning. Politically, we would hope to convince a broad spectrum of political opinion about the desirability of protection. Intellectually, we are intimidated by the task of re-inventing socialist collectivism which is a large project. Nevertheless, our view is that the break with free trade is a necessary but not sufficient condition for the regeneration of British manufacturing. With this qualification registered, it is possible to turn to the argument for protection as a means of easing the foreign trade constraint.

Economists rest the case for free trade on theory about the capitalist economy in general. We would begin to argue the case for protection by examining the character of the current British trade problem. It is the sectoral and geographic composition of the British manufacturing trade deficit which determines our preference for selective import controls. Of course, there is a general problem about poor British performance in manufacturing trade. The manufacturing capability of all the advanced countries rests on their engineering sector; as a NEDO (1984) paper shows, this sector accounts for 40 to 65 per cent of the exports of all the advanced countries. Across this broad central sector, British manufacturing performance is inferior; in comparison with other leading industrial countries, British engineering exports account for a lower proportion of all exports, import penetration is higher on the home market and the British only achieve a small engineering trade surplus relative to home demand (NEDO, 1984, pp. 17–19). At the same time it is important to emphasise that this general weakness rests on a more specific sectoral failure. The British manufacturing trade deficit is the result of a two-commodity, two-country problem; it is largely caused by the trade in motor vehicles and electronics with West Germany and Japan.

Table 4.12 shows the sectoral importance of road vehicles and

Table 4.12   Manufacturing trade deficit

	Deficit [1] (£ million)		
		1983	
	Total	*Road vehicles*	*Electronics* [2]
Imports	44,905	5,754	7,743
Exports	39,919	3,084	5,331
Crude balance	− 4,986	− 2,670	− 2,412
		1984	
	Total	*Road vehicles*	*Electronics* [2]
Imports	52,886	5,958	9,809
Exports	46,668	3,312	6,967
Crude balance	− 6,216	− 2,646	− 2,842

[1] The total trade deficits in this Table do not agree exactly with those shown elsewhere in this chapter. The Overseas Trade Statistics deficit is calculated in a slightly different way from that which appears in the Balance of Payments (Pink Book).
[2] Electronics includes telecommunications and sound recording equipment, office machines and automatic data processing equipment, plus electrical machinery, apparatus and equipment n.e.s.
Source: Overseas Trade Statistics, December 1983 and 1984

consumer electronics. The overall British manufacturing trade deficit is largely accounted for by trade in these two product areas; in 1984 they accounted for £5.5 billion out of the overall trade deficit of £6.2 billion. The deepening trade crisis is mainly caused by the changing balance between exports and imports in these two sectors. The trade in cars shows us the classic de-industrialisation pattern of a steady secular rise of imports followed somewhat later by a collapse of exports. In 1973 the UK was still a net exporter of cars to the extent of 94,000 vehicles; a decade later the British were net importers to the extent of 802,000 vehicles. Over this period, import volume had more than doubled from 505,000 to 1,076,000 cars and export volumes had more than halved from 599,000 to 274,000. British car exports held up reasonably well in the 1970s and, after a slight recovery, stood at 570,000 in 1977 but they have fallen away rapidly since 1978. In cars (as in consumer electronics) this kind of trade pattern is the outward sign of industrial collapse from a position of relative strength; in consumer electronics, imports of foreign kits have largely replaced domestic manufacture and the car industry is well down this road.

Japan and West Germany are the two countries which supply most of our imported motor vehicles and consumer electronic goods. In its evidence to the Lords Select Committee, the Department of Trade and Industry indicated that the trade deficit with Japan had risen from £960 million in 1979 to £2,654 in 1983. The commodity composition of that deficit was not analysed. But when this is done, it is clear that 80 per cent of the Japanese deficit is attributable to the two key sectors; £1364 million of the deficit arises in electronics and £721 million in road vehicles. Our trade with Japan is largely a one-way traffic in these two kinds of products. The Department of Trade and Industry also indicated that Britain had a manufacturing trade deficit with the EEC which rose from £3,081 in 1979 to £7,914 million in 1983. Rather disingenuously, the Department did not break down the deficit by country of origin. When this is done, it is clear that 62 per cent of our overall EEC trade deficit in 1983 arose from trade with West Germany. We have a German trade problem, but we do not otherwise have an overwhelming European trade problem. In 1983 our trade with Italy and France was more or less in balance; in that year, Italy accounted for only 15 per cent of our overall EEC trade deficit and France for just 14 per cent. The commodity composition of our manufacturing trade deficit with West Germany is again interesting; whereas motor vehicles account for only 40 per cent of our trade deficit with Japan, they account for a massive 60 per cent of our trade deficit with West Germany where cars alone account for half the deficit. Trade with West Germany has never been a one-way traffic; in 1980 the West Germans supplied 16 per cent of our manufactured imports and took 9 per cent of our manufactured exports (Williams *et al.*, 1983, pp. 112–15). But a major imbalance has arisen as the British import increasing numbers of German cars which of course have a high individual unit value.

Classical economic theory used a two-country, two-commodity, two-factor model to construct the general case for free trade; our more empirical two-country, two-commodity analysis of the problem can be used to justify protection in Britain now. General import controls are unnecessary because selective import controls on a few products from a couple of countries would avert the coming trade crisis. Incidentally such controls would make it possible to undertake Keynesian reflation which is impossible as long as any injected purchasing power sooner or later leaks abroad via consumer purchases of German and Japanese cars and consumer electronics. At the same time, it would be irresponsible to argue the case for selective import controls without briefly discussing the form which such protection should take. In our view, selective import controls in motor vehicles and consumer electronics should be primarily based on value-added content regulation rather than on an extensive apparatus of tariffs and quotas. Higher domestic content in British manufactured products would be rewarded with a variety of tax privileges for purchasers and users of these products; imports with a negligible British content and assembled products with a low British content would be penalised. The virtue of such content regulations is that they can not only correct a temporary imbalance by blocking imports but also create conditions under which it is at least possible for domestic manufacturers to replace imports.

The specific nature of the content regulations should be tailored to the circumstances of particular British industries. In a memorandum submitted to the Commons Select Committee on car components (Williams, and Haslam, 1985), we have indicated how content regulation might be applied to the car industry where fragmented demand encourages imports and assembly of foreign kits and discourages manufacture because small volumes do not allow manufacturers to recoup the costs of development. Half the cars sold in the UK are now supplied by Ford and GM and the UK content of the cars which Ford and GM sell in Britain has declined precipitously over the past decade: from 1973 to 1983 the UK content of all Vauxhalls sold declined from 89 to 26 per cent and the UK content of all Fords sold declined from 85 to 43 per cent (Jones, 1985). This slump in British content occurred because British manufactured cars were replaced by imports and by kits of foreign-sourced parts which were only assembled in British factories. Any content regulation policy should deal not only with the imports but also with the kit cars. Kit cars are preferable to imports in that up to 60 per cent of the value-added originates in the British factories where the cars are assembled and bulky components like tyres, glass and bumpers are locally manufactured; the benefits of this are significant because approximately 70 per cent of the British value-added is paid out in wages to British workers. But the assembly of kit cars does not ease the foreign trade constraint; in fact it locks us into importing because any expansion of British domestic demand will draw in more foreign kits which are absolutely necessary to British production.

For this reason, the value-added content policy for cars should defend a concentrated domestic car manufacturing industry rather than encourage a dispersed assembly industry. A sliding scale of discrimination starting at a low level around 50 per cent will inevitably encourage dispersed assembly; in this situation the European majors, the American multinationals and the Japanese are adept at getting round the political opposition to imports by setting up small satellite assembly operations which are profitable at model volumes of 50,000 per annum or less. If we are concerned to defend the existing manufacturing base, the proper policy is to have a sharp discrimination between cars which have British content of more than 80 per cent and those which have less. Two firms (Austin and Ford) have four factories (Longbridge, Cowley, Dagenham and Halewood) which can all produce an 80 per cent British motor car (Metro, Maestro/Montego, Escort, Sierra). All of these factories have been completely re-equipped and re-tooled in the period since 1980 and now embody more than

£2,500 million of recent investment. Austin Rover and Ford jointly have excess capacity of some 600,000 which is divided roughly equally between the two firms (*Financial Times*, 12 January 1985; Jones, 1985). Appropriate content regulations could load the four remaining car factories with throughput and prevent the surplus capacity being scrapped and/or used for assembly operations.

If selective import controls are an appropriate response to Britain's present predicament, it must be conceded that the doctrine of free trade is well-entrenched. It is therefore necessary to confront the range of orthodox intellectual and political objections to protectionism. We will begin by noting that the economist's theoretical case for free trade is vulnerable at several different levels. Its conclusions about maximising world output depend on a number of unrealised (and unrealisable) assumptions about the mobility of factors, the full employment of resources and instantaneous automatic processes for correcting imbalances. It also requires either (and ideally) no institutional organisations at all, or institutions run with extraordinary wisdom and self-denial. Apart from all this, orthodox theory rests on intellectual sleight of hand because nations do not figure at all as actors in its reassuring syllogisms; its welfare-maximising conclusions jump from the maximisation of individual utility functions to the maximising of world output. As List insisted over a century ago, the classical theory necessarily leaves out any explicit treatment of the national interest. From a national point of view, free trade raises a whole series of crucial issues which are not addressed in orthodox theory: how are the undoubted gains from trade shared between nations; and what is there to prevent the long-run economic structure of nations being determined by short-run considerations of comparative advantage? This last issue is a perennial one. In List's times, Britain's industrial advantage was so great that under free trade much of continental Europe would have been forced to concentrate on primary production. In our times, the Japanese manufacturing advantage is so great that under free trade the Japanese would monopolise large areas of manufacturing and that would leave the other advanced countries with a very peculiar economic structure.

In practice, of course, free trade is the doctrine of the international winners at any particular time and protection is the refuge of starters and losers. List shrewdly remarked that he too would have been a free trader if he had been English. But not, of course, if he had been English in the autarchic 1930s or the deflationary 1980s when the national interest would be best served by protection. When we encounter resistance to our arguments in the 1980s it may be worth recalling that the original and radical generation of liberal collectivists did accept the case for protection in the circumstances of the 1930s. Let Keynes speak for himself:

I am no longer a free trader – and I believe that practically no
one else is – in the old sense of the term to the extent of believing
in a very high degree of national specialisation and in abandoning
any industry which is unable for the time being to hold its own.
Where wages are immobile, this would be an extraordinarily
dangerous doctrine to follow. I believe, for example, that this
country is in the long run reasonably adapted for, and ought
always to have, a motor industry, a steel industry, a farming
industry. If it is proved to me that in present circumstances and at
present wages these industries cannot live, I am in favour of
protecting them. But a real free trader would answer without
hesitation – let them go. (Keynes, 1982, pp. 379–80)

As the quotation shows, Keynes was primarily concerned with the
problems of internal cost adjustment (and especially the requirement
for wage reductions) which might be forced upon debtor countries who
were trying to recover international competitiveness. He conceived the
problem of adjustment in orthodox price/cost terms and his arguments
were set in a particular historical context which was defined by the
failure of internal adjustment after Britain's return to gold in 1925.
But if we were to generalise his argument the position is quite clear;
debtor countries with payments problems and (cost) competitiveness
difficulties should not be asked to bear a deflationary or de-indu-
strialising burden of adjustment. If this adjustment was being forced
upon them, (tariff) protection was the proper response.

In his 1940s work on the creation of a post-war international
economic system, Keynes was developing rather than renouncing his
earlier positions. A liberal international order of free trade would
be best for all, but only if the international community created
institutions which would protect debtor countries from 'the social
strain of an adjustment downwards' (Keynes, 1980a, p. 28). As
Keynes said in 1944 in a speech in advance of the Bretton Woods
negotiations,

We will not accept deflation at the dictate of influences from
outside. In other words we abjure the instruments of Bank Rate
and Credit contraction operating through the increase of
unemployment as a means of forcing our domestic economy into
line with external factors. (Keynes, 1980b, p. 16)

Again Keynes conceived the problems in an orthodox way; international loans would deal with temporary payments problems and
changes in exchange rates could resolve fundamental disequilibria.
But the implications of Keynes's position are clear. If a resurrected
Keynes were to survey our present international institutions, the

international problem of massive and permanent trade disequilibria, and the impending British trade crisis, there can be no doubt that he would recommend effective protection as a means of evading deflationary adjustment.

So far, we have argued that the theory of free trade is incredible and it has never been accepted uncritically as a practical guide to national policy, even by impeccable liberal collectivists. If these points are accepted, economists can only resist protection with the pragmatic argument that in our present national circumstances protectionism would diminish producer efficiency and consumer welfare.

But it is free trade (not protection) which is undermining producer efficiency in Britain now. As markets fragment and import penetration increases, British enterprises face a limited market which prevents them using their capital equipment efficiently. Austin Rover is not the only firm in this kind of predicament; the British Steel Corporation has a total 26 million tonne capacity, but it only mans 14.3 million tonnes and in 1983 produced just 11.7 million tonnes of steel (Williams and Haslam, 1986b). The development of 'flexible manufacturing' will not abolish this problem because, as the Japanese show, the economies of scope are most effectively exploited by those who also aggressively pursue scale. As for the consumer welfare benefits of trade, they were of course considerable when European manufactures were being exchanged for the rest of the world's primaries in the early twentieth century. But it would be more difficult to argue that large increases in welfare are obtained by the interchange of manufactures which has developed amongst the advanced countries since 1945. In most cases, the consumer-good trade is in differentiated products which are separated by minor packaging differences. Of course the British consumer can recognise and prefer the Japanese TV, German hatchback or Italian washing machine. But it is hard to argue that (s)he would suffer a serious loss of welfare if forced for a time to accept the substitute British product. Consumers elsewhere in the advanced countries do accept restrictions on their choice with equanimity; there are few protests from the Italian consumers who are denied Japanese cars and effectively encouraged to buy Fiats.

In fact, the more serious pragmatic economic arguments based on our current circumstances all point in a protectionist direction. There are persistent differences in the manufacturing capability of the advanced industrial countries which natural adjustment mechanisms cannot resolve. This point emerges very clearly from the discussion of the Japanese cost advantage in motor car production. If the yen appreciated from 215 to the $ to 185 to the $, Altshuler *et al.* (1984) argued there would still be a substantial Japanese cost advantage in car production. No appreciation of the yen would produce a proportionate increase in Japanese export prices because many items

needed in Japanese production can be purchased with non-yen currencies earned in profitable export sales. Under these conditions, free
trade is a system for exporting jobs to Japan. The success of Japanese
enterprises depends on the displacement of Western producers in
product lines like cars, steel and consumer electronics. With new
products, the Japanese succeed by bidding for a share of the Western
consumer-spend with their novelties. This system diverts rather than
creates purchasing power because it does not create its own demand at
a macro international level; it funnels demand to Japan and establishes
payments constraints elswhere. If these arguments are acceptable or
obvious in the Japanese case, why are the British so reluctant to extend
them to the West German case? If every advanced country needs
protection from the Japanese, surely the least successful advanced
country also needs protection from the Germans?

If the economic logic of our arguments is accepted, it is still possible
to resist protection on the grounds that it is politically impossible or
unwise for Britain to set up selective import controls. These arguments
should be considered seriously because in many ways they carry
more weight than the rationalisations of the economists. It would
be irresponsible for one country to set up trade restrictions which
subsequently triggered a general downward spiral in international
trade and a movement towards autarchy. We may have reservations
about the benefits from the interchange of manufactures but we have
no doubts that a disorderly retreat into autarchy would be exceedingly
disruptive for all the advanced countries. We cannot see how British
action could provoke such dire consequences. Britain accounts for not
much more than 7 per cent of world manufactured exports and
perhaps 10 per cent of manufactured imports; selective import controls
on cars and consumer electronics would apply to only part of our
import trade. It could indeed be argued that international crisis and
a general breakdown of the trade system is brought nearer if deficit-
running minor nations are prevented from adopting moderate protectionist remedies. If selective import controls are not irresponsible,
many would argue that they are impracticable because they expose
us to the risk of retaliation from major trading partners. On this view
it is simply impossible to break the free trade rules of the game which
Britain has accepted by virtue of membership in such organisations
as the General Agreement on Trade and Tariffs, the International
Monetary Fund and the European Economic Community. But, like
the other advanced countries, we have complete freedom to set
national controls on imports from Japan; under EEC rules, member
countries individually determine their tariff and quota policies on
Japanese cars and consumer electronics. Retaliation is no problem
when the Japanese import virtually nothing from Britain. It is Germany which is the problem. Controls on imports from Germany would

break the rules of the EEC free trade area and the Germans, like our other European partners, are in a position to retaliate. Much would depend on how the case for British import controls was presented. It would be politically crucial to identify the problem as a German problem which required corrective action which would not harm our other European partners who themselves, to a lesser extent, suffer from free trade with West Germany. It should also be pointed out that none of our European trading partners has a long-run interest in the impoverishment of the British national economy which is still the third largest in Europe for many producer and consumer goods. Politics is not about rational argument and so retaliation may be a real problem. But at this stage, when the debate about import controls is being opened, retaliation is mainly an intellectual big stick which the doctrinaire free trader waves about when he has lost all the other arguments. As such, it should not be taken too seriously.

After a long discussion of the British economic crisis and its resolution, we turn finally to a brief examination of social policy. This order and emphasis is quite deliberate. We have postponed any discussion of new initiatives in social policy because the fundamental point we want to make is that we do not see much possibility for such initiatives unless we use planning and protectionism to solve our economic problems.

We do not believe that radical social policy should be or is a kind of luxury which is paid for out of the surplus of economic prosperity. There is no automatic connection between the attainment of prosperity and new social policy initiatives. But economic crisis and slump does effectively constrain such initiatives. Thus, in Britain in the late 1980s, unless something is done about the impending foreign trade crisis, the government will not have the revenue to maintain existing programmes let alone make new initiatives. The government is now heavily dependent on oil revenue; in 1984–5 £12 billion or 12 per cent of all government revenue came from North Sea oil. To put that £12 billion into perspective, it equals 37 per cent of 1984–5 income tax revenue or 65 per cent of VAT revenue. As Table 4.13 shows, the

Table 4.13 Official forecasts of British government oil revenue

	£ billion
1985	13.5
1986	11.0
1987	8.5
1988	7.5
1989	7.3
1990	7.1

Source: Chancellor's 1985 Budget Statement

official projections are that oil revenue will decline sharply by the end of the decade.

The official projections show oil revenue halved by the end of the decade. This is on an assumption of an oil price of $28 a barrel and a $ versus £ exchange rate of 1.11; if the price of oil sags or currencies shift adversely, then oil revenues could fall away faster. The decline in North Sea oil production is in itself enough to produce a fiscal crisis unless the government is prepared to make substantial increases in direct and indirect taxation. This fiscal crisis will be intensified insofar as a rising manufacturing trade deficit creates payments problems before the oil runs down to the point of self-sufficiency. In this situation, orthodox policies of deflation will depress output and raise unemployment simultaneously diminishing the tax base and increasing the requirement for government expenditure on social security benefits. At this point, any government is likely to be under pressure to cut essential services and raise tax rates.

The stage is therefore set for a new phase of social policy in the context of economic decline and crisis. In this new phase liberal collectivism can play its last and least heroic role. The political ideology developed by Keynes and Beveridge was initially used more than forty years ago to argue the case for radical new welfare-augmenting initiatives in the sphere of the economic and the social. In a different context of economic decline liberal collectivism is now being used officially in the 1980s to support the case for welfare-diminishing cuts in the sphere of the social.

This can be illustrated by referring to the current debate on the abolition of SERPS – the state's earnings-related pension scheme which was introduced by a Labour government in 1975. The key official document here is the government's Green Paper *Reform of Social Security* (1985a). This contained proposals for the abolition of SERPS which the government has since abandoned. In the face of widespread criticism of the Green Paper proposals, the government has decided to 'reform' rather than abolish SERPS. From our point of view this does not really matter because what we want to demonstrate is that the government's original proposals for abolishing SERPS were cast entirely in a liberal collectivist form which would have been familiar to Beveridge.

The Green Paper tackled the question of what old age pension provision should be made apart from the flat-rate national insurance provision which is to remain unchanged in liberal collectivist terms 'as an entitlement earned by people from paying National Insurance Contributions' (*Reform of Social Security*, 1985a, vol. 2, p. 3). In this case, the issue becomes, what form should supplementary earnings-related provision take? The existing SERPS scheme in this field was criticised on grounds of 'cost' which was conceived of in liberal collectivist terms as a matter of direct state expenditure; the Green Paper did not set such direct expenditure in the context of 'tax expenditures' which are so crucial in the parallel world of occupational pensions. But, at the same time, the Green Paper argued for good ideological reasons that the question of cost was subsidiary to 'the fundamental question, of whether pension provision cannot be provided in a different and better way' (*Reform of Social Security*, 1985a, vol. 2, p. 21). Above the state minimum, existing provision takes the form of occupational pensions plus the SERPS scheme which covers nearly half of the workforce. The 'better way' proposed in the Green Paper was to take the form of occupational pensions plus 'personal pensions'. In the personal pension both employer and employee would have contributed to fund not a group scheme, but an individual pension plan which would be portable in the sense that the employee could take his pension with him when he changed employer. Under the Green Paper proposals, the state was to be evicted from the field of earnings-related pensions and this was justified on impeccably liberal collectivist grounds; 'it is preferable for individuals to make provision themselves during their working lives to supplement the basic pension, than for the responsibility to be left wholly to the state' (*Reform of Social Security*, 1985a, vol. 2, p. 4). If these proposals had been enacted, the state would have been returned to its proper role as the provider of a basic social security minimum.

If the ideology was classic, the novelty was that the 'reform' proposed in the Green Paper offered very little to the next generation of pensioners. The promise was that under the proposed new regime, workers would have the choice between individualised and portable pensions or occupational pension schemes. But half the population are not enrolled in occupational pension schemes so that they do not have any choice but to accept whatever fall-back provision is made available by government fiat; the Hobson's choice of personal pensions was being offered to the vast majority of manual workers in smaller private firms. To add insult to injury the fall-back personal pension proposed was hardly worth having unless employee and employer made additional voluntary contributions. The compulsory contribution levels for portable pensions were set very low. For personal pensions the proposed employer and employee contributions were each 2 per cent of salary; by way of contrast, the employer's contribution to staff schemes averaged over 12 per cent. Under any scheme, low contribution rates buy low benefits and this was particularly so under the Green Paper proposals because the personal pension was to be of the money purchase type (i.e. determined by what contributions and investment income will buy when annuitised); by way of contrast more than 95 per cent of occupational pension schemes are of the 'final salary' type (i.e. the fund pays a proportion of earnings at the end of the scheme member's working life). The disadvantage of money purchase schemes is overwhelming because when, as in the 1970s, the return on investment does not keep up with inflation then the value of the additional pension is reduced.

Just as Keynes could hardly be enrolled as a dogmatic free trader of the modern type, so Beveridge can hardly be enlisted as the prototype of this kind of liberal collectivism. In many ways, the Green Paper represents a kind of pathological coarsening and degeneration of his liberal collectivism. To begin with, the Green Paper has a dogmatic preference for private pension provision. Beveridge's position (as in the critique of industrial assurance) was that if the market produced irrational results then state intervention was necessary. And the proposals for personal pensions were irrational in Beveridge's terms. In 1983 the administrative costs of life insurance and (group) pension funds account for 20 per cent of the £16.6 billion pensions and benefits paid out (*Financial Times*, 8 June 1985). If *individual* schemes became the norm, the expenses of selling and administration would undoubtedly be much higher. In a response to the government proposals, the CBI argued that the administrative costs associated with investing the individual's contributions in long-term securities were such that minimum contributions would only be deposited with banks and building societies (*Reform of Social Security*, 1985a, vol. 2, p. 4). It is also virtually certain that if the personal pensions proposals had been enacted, the ultimate beneficiaries would have got less for more. Under the pre-1985 *status quo*, employees who were outside occupational schemes were, with their employers, paying a national insurance contribution of 19.45 per cent; under the Green Paper proposals the effective replacement contribution rate would have been 20.5 per cent (a reduced insurance contribution of 16.5 per cent plus the compulsory personal pension contribution of 4 per cent). This marginally increased contribution would have earned perhaps less than half the current state earnings-related pension entitlement (*Reform of Social Security*, 1985a, vol. 2, pp. 8, 16). Even the occupational pension scheme members get less for more because they would have paid an increased rate of national insurance contribution (up from 13.5 to 16.5 per cent) and lost state inflation proofing of the guaranteed minimum pension (GMP) part of the employer's pension.

Hegel was correct when he observed that all historic facts and personages occur twice: thus Beveridge and the White Paper of 1942 becomes Fowler and the Green Paper of 1985. But Marx's dictum, the first time as tragedy and the second time as farce, does not apply here. In the case of liberal collectivist ideology, the first time round it was a progressive justification and the second time a reactionary excuse. The original achievement of liberal collectivism in the 1940s was that it established a new terrain for economic and social policy because it insisted progressively on the necessity for new minimum standards in employment and income maintenance albeit with the maximum play for capitalist freedoms. As we have argued throughout this book, the happy combination of minimalist intervention and capitalist freedom was always problematic and cannot now be sustained. When it is reiterated in the 1980s, the ideology of liberal collectivism simply compromises any chance of decent income and secure employment for many working people.

Bibliography

(*References are limited to works which have been directly used in the text.*)

Abernathy, W., Clark, K. and Kantrow, A. (1981), 'The new industrial competition', *Harvard Business Review*, September–October, pp. 68–81.

Altshuler, A., Anderson, M., Jones, D., Roos, D. and Womack, J. (1984), *The Future of the Automobile*, London, Allen & Unwin.

Annual Abstracts (1970–85), Central Statistical Office, London, HMSO.

Atkinson, J. (1984), 'Manning or uncertainty', mimeo, Brighton Institute of Manpower Studies.

Bank of England Quarterly Bulletin (1985), 'Services in the UK economy', September, pp. 404–14.

Beveridge, W. (1942), *Social Insurance and Allied Services*, London, HMSO.

Beveridge, W. (1944), *Full Employment in a Free Society*, London, Allen & Unwin.

Beveridge, W. (1948), *Voluntary Action*, London, Allen & Unwin.

Beveridge, Lord and Wells, A. (eds.) (1949), *The Evidence for Voluntary Action*, London, Allen & Unwin.

Board of Inland Revenue (1983), *Cost of Tax Reliefs for Pension Schemes: Appropriate Statistical Approaches*, London, HMSO.

Boston Consulting Group (1975), *Strategy Alternatives for the British Motorcycle Industry*, London, HMSO.

British Labour Statistics: Historical Abstract 1886–1968 (1971), Department of Employment, London, HMSO.

Census of Employment (1971, 1981), Department of Employment, London, HMSO.

Census of Population (1901–1981), Office of Population Censuses and Surveys, London, HMSO.

Central Policy Review Staff (1975), *The Future of the Car Industry*, London, HMSO.

Central Statistical Office (1984), *UK National Accounts, 1984*, London, HMSO.

Charter for Jobs (1985), *We Can Cut Employment*, London, Charter for Jobs.

Cohen, J. (chairman) (1934), *Report of the Committee on Industrial Assurance and Assurance on the Lives of Children under Ten Years of Age*, London, HMSO.

Cole, R. (1972), 'Permanent employment in Japan: facts and fantasies', *Industrial and Labor Relations Review*, vol. 26, pp. 615–30.

Confederation of British Industry (1985), *Response to the Green Paper on the Reform of Social Security*, London, CBI.

Cutler, A., Hindess, B., Hirst, P. and Hussain, A. (1978), *Marx's Capital and Capitalism Today*, vol. 2, London, Routledge & Kegan Paul.

Daly, A., Hitchens, D. and Wagner, K. (1985), 'Productivity, machinery and skills in a sample of British and German manufacturing plants', *National Institute Economic Review*, February, pp. 48–62.

Dex, S. (1984), *Women's Work Histories: An Analysis of the Women and Employment Survey*, London, Department of Employment (Research Paper no. 46).

154

Dow, J. C. R. (1964), *The Management of the British Economy 1945–60*, Cambridge, Cambridge University Press.

Economic Trends (1985), Central Statistical Office, London, HMSO.

Employment Gazette (1984), 'Unemployment and ethnic origin', London, HMSO, June.

Employment Gazette (1985), 'Pension scheme membership in 1983', London, Department of Employment, December, pp. 494–7.

Employment Gazette (various dates), London, Department of Employment.

Employment Policy (1944), White Paper, London, HMSO.

Esso Magazine (1984), 'United Kingdom energy outlook', Supplement, 1983–4.

Fetherston, M., Moore, B. and Rhodes, J. (1977), 'Manufacturing export shares and cost competitiveness of advanced industrial countries', *Economic Policy Review* (Cambridge Department of Applied Economics), no. 3, pp. 62–70.

Garvin, D. (1983), 'Quality on the line', *Harvard Business Review*, September–October, pp. 65–75.

General Household Survey (1976), Office of Population Censuses and Surveys, London, HMSO.

Gershuny, J. and Miles, I. (1983), *The New Service Economy*, London, Frances Pinter.

Glyn, A. (1985), *A Million Jobs a Year*, London, Verso.

Godley, W. (1986), 'A doomed economy', *New Society*, 17 January 1986.

Government Actuaries Department (1981), *Occupational Pension Schemes 1979* (6th survey), London, HMSO.

Hakin, C. (1979), *Occupational Segregation: A Comparative Study of the Degree and Pattern of the Differentiation Between Men and Women's Work in Britain, the United States and Other Countries*, London, Department of Employment (Research Paper no. 9).

Hall, R. E. (1982), 'The importance of lifetime jobs in the US economy', *American Economic Review*, September, pp. 16–24.

Hall. R. W. (1983), *Zero Inventories*, Homewood, Illinois, Dow-Jones Irwin.

House of Lords Select Committee on Overseas Trade (1985), *Report and Minutes of Evidence*, London, HMSO.

ILO Yearbook of Labour Statistics (1950–85), Geneva, ILO.

James, C. (1984), *Occupational Pensions: the Failure of Occupational Welfare*, Fabian Tract no. 497, London, Fabian Society.

Jones, D. T. (1985), 'The import threat to the UK car industry', Brighton, Science Policy Research Unit.

Juran, J. (1978), 'Japanese and Western quality: a contrast in methods and results', *Management Review*, November, pp. 26–45.

Kahn, R. F. (1931), 'The relation of home investment to unemployment', *Economic Journal*, vol. XLI.

Keegan, W. (1985), *Britain Without Oil*, Harmondsworth, Penguin.

Kendal, W. (1984), 'Why Japanese workers work', *Management Today*, January, pp. 72–95.

Kennedy, J. C. (1973), 'Employment Policy', in Robinson, J. (ed.), *After Keynes*, pp. 71–87, Oxford, Blackwell.

Keynes, J. M. (1936), *The General Theory of Employment, Interest and Money*, London, Macmillan.

Keynes, J. M. (1940), *How to Pay for the War*, London, Macmillan.

Keynes, J. M. (1978), *Collected Works*, vol. XXII, London, Macmillan.

Keynes, J. M. (1980a), *Collected Works*, vol. XXV, London, Macmillan.

Keynes, J. M. (1980b), *Collected Works*, vol. XXVI, London, Macmillan.

Keynes, J. M. (1982), *Collected Works*, vol. XX, London, Macmillan.

Labour Force Survey (1983), 'The unemployed: survey estimates for 1983 compared with the monthly count', *Employment Gazette*, August 1984.

Labour Research (1985), *Farewell to Welfare*, London, Labour Research.

Le Grand, J. (1983), *The Strategy of Equality*, London, Heinemann.

Macmillan, H. (1937), *The Middle Way*, London, Macmillan.

156 *Bibliography*

Magaziner, I. and Hout, T. M. (1980), *Japanese Industrial Policy*, London, Policy Studies Institute.
Magaziner, I. and Reich, R. (1982), *Minding America's Business*, New York, Harcourt Brace.
Martin, J. and Roberts, C. (1984), *Women and Employment: A Lifetime Perspective*, Social Survey Report SS1143, London, HMSO.
Memorandum by Ministers on Certain Proposals Relative to Unemployment (1929), BPP 1928–9, Cmnd. 3331, vol. XVI, 873.
Millard Tucker, J. (chairman) (1954), *Report of the Committee on the Taxation Treatment of Provision for Retirement*, Cmnd. 9063, London, HMSO.
Moylan, S., Millar, J. and Davies, R. (1984), *For Richer, For Poorer*, DHSS Cohort Study of Unemployed Men, London, HMSO (DHSS Research Report no. 11).
National Association of Pension Funds (1984), *Survey of Occupational Pensions 1983*, London, NAPF.
National Consumer Council (1984), *Of Benefit to All*, London, National Consumer Council.
National Economic Development Office (1984), *Trade Patterns and Industrial Change*, London, NEDO.
New Earnings Survey (1980, 1983, 1984), Department of Employment, London, HMSO.
Office of Population Censuses and Surveys (1974), *Occupational Mortality, 1970–2*, London, HMSO.
Office of Population Censuses and Surveys (1985), *Monitor*, GHS/1, London, HMSO.
Organisation for Economic Cooperation and Development (1984), *Japan*, Paris, OECD.
Overseas Trade Statistics (1970–85), Department of Trade and Industry, London, HMSO.
Piore, M. and Sabell, C. (1984), *The Second Industrial Divide*, New York, Basic Books.
Popay, J., Rimmer, L. and Rossiter, C. (1982), 'One parent families and employment', *Employment Gazette*, December, pp. 531–5.
Reddin, M. and Pilch, M. (1985), *Can We Afford Our Future?*, London, Age Concern.
Reform of Social Security (Green Paper) (1985a), vol. 1, Cmnd. 9517, vol. 2, *Programme for Change*, Cmnd. 9518, vol. 3, *Background Papers*, Cmnd. 9519, London, HMSO.
Reform of Social Security (White Paper) (1985b), Cmnd. 9691, London, HMSO.
Roberts, B. C. and Smith, J. H. (eds) (1966), *Manpower Policy and Employment Trends*, London, LSE and George Bell.
Robinson, O. and Wallace, J. (1982), 'Part-time employment in Great Britain', preliminary memorandum in House of Lords Select Committee on the European Communities, 19th Report, Session 1981–2, Voluntary Part-time Work, H.L. 216, London HMSO.
Robinson, O. and Wallace, J. (1984), 'Part-time employment and sex discrimination legislation in GB', London, Department of Employment (Research Paper no. 43).
Robson, C. (1982), *Metro*, Cambridge, Patrick Stephens.
Schonberger, R. (1982), *Japanese Manufacturing Techniques*, New York, Free Press.
Smith, K. (1984), *Britain's Economic Crisis*, Harmondsworth, Penguin.
Social Trends (1986), Central Statistical Office, London, HMSO.
Society of Motor Manufacturers and Traders (1984), *The Motor Industry of Great Britain*, London, SMMT.
Titmuss, R. (1976), *Essays on the Welfare State*, London.
UK Balance of Payments (1964–84), Central Statistical Office, London, HMSO.
White Paper on Employment Policy (1944), London, HMSO.
Williams, K. (1984), 'Made in USA', *Economy and Society*, vol. 13, no. 4.
Williams, K. and Haslam, C. (1985), 'The decline of manufacturing and the shift to assembly in the car industry' (memorandum submitted to the Commons Select Committee on Motor Vehicle Components).

Williams, K. and Haslam, C. (1986a), 'An obituary for Austin Rover', *Account,* 23 January 1986.

Williams, K. and Haslam, C. (1986b) (with Williams, J. and Wardlow, A.), Accounting for failure in nationalised industries', *Economy and Society,* vol. 15, no. 2.

Williams, K., Williams, J. and Haslam, C. (1986), *The Breakdown of Austin Rover,* Aldershot, Gower.

Williams, K., Williams, J. and Thomas, D. (1983), *Why Are the British Bad at Manufacturing?,* London, Routledge & Kegan Paul.

Willis, J. and Hardwick, P. (1978), *Tax Expenditure in the United Kingdom,* London, Heinemann.

Willman, P. (1984), 'The reform of collective bargaining and strike action in BL cars 1976–82', *Industrial Relations Journal,* vol. 15, no, 2.

Willman, P. and Winch, C, (1984), *Technological Change, Management Strategy and Industrial Relations,* Cambridge, Cambridge University Press.

Wilson, A. and Levy, H. (1937), *Industrial Assurance,* London, Oxford University Press.

Index